Survey of
Metaphysics
and Esoterism

Frithjof Schuon

with a foreword by Bruce K. Hanson

World Wisdom Books, Inc.

First published as two books:
Résumé de Métaphysique Intégrale
Le Courrier du Livre, Paris, 1985
and
Sur les Traces de la Religion Pérenne
Le Courrier du Livre, Paris, 1982

Survey of Metaphysics and Esoterism
© 2000 Estate of Frithjof Schuon

The cover design is the sacred syllable *Om*

Library of Congress Cataloging-in-Publication Data

Schuon, Frithjof, 1907-1998
    [Résumé de métaphysique intégrale. English]
    Survey of metaphysics and esoterism / Frithjof Schuon ; with a foreword by
Bruce K. Hanson.
      p. cm. — (The library of traditional wisdom)
    Includes bibliographical references and index.
    ISBN 0-941532-27-5
    1. Metaphysics—Miscellanea. 2. Religion—Miscellanea. I. Schuon, Frithjof,
1907-1998 Sur les traces de la religion pérenne. English. II. Title. III. Series.
    BF1999 .S361213   2000
    299'.93—dc21   99-054307

Printed in The United States of America
on acid-free paper

For information address World Wisdom Books, Inc.
P. O. Box 2682, Bloomington, Indiana 47402-2682
http://www.worldwisdom.com

Table of Contents

Foreword

There is a story told by the Chinese sage Mencius of a large mountain outside a city, a mountain whose original luxuriously forested state had been obscured and long since forgotten after years of logging and grazing. To look at the mountain now, people would never guess its original condition. Mencius intends this story as a metaphor for the human condition. He was telling the people that, after years of acquired conditioning, through a mindless absorption of the times, they too had forgotten their own original state.

It is precisely this recalling of each of us to our original nature that lies at the heart of religion. And it is this reminder to "become that which we are" that lies at the heart of Frithjof Schuon's writings as well. Schuon, through more than a score of books written over more than half a century, has sought to keep alive the vision of the *Sophia Perennis* wherein "[O]ur soul proves God because it is proportioned to the divine Nature. . . . And it is in these foundations of human nature — image of the divine Nature — that the *religio perennis* is rooted, and with it all religion and all wisdom" (4). We humans each carry the truth and light of the Absolute within the depths of our being. And this light, Schuon points out, "reminds [each one of us] of what he is, and of what he should be since he has forgotten what he is" (82).

To speak of "becoming what we are" suggests a distinction that must be made as carefully as possible. For just as most of us confuse intensity of feeling with clarity of thought, so too

v

do we often confuse *being* human and *becoming* human. At the level of being we are, of course, human; which is to say, every child who is born of human parents comes into the world with a human essence. But it is quite another matter to *achieve* our humanity in our existence; that is, to realize to the fullest degree the very promise which already is our nature. As the saying goes, there is many a slip between the cup and the lip.

Now "becoming human" is necessarily a conscious task. We don't automatically grow into our humanity. "Man is called upon to choose," Schuon tells us, and in fact, "the very reason for being of the human condition is to choose, and to make the right choice" (75). This certainly distinguishes us from creatures non-human. An acorn does not choose to fulfill its destiny as an oak, nor does a kitten need to find the will to embody its vocation. We humans are the creatures that can fail to become what we already are by nature; and, it might be added, we regularly do so. "[O]ne wants to be oneself without wanting to be so altogether, hence without wanting to go beyond the empirical ego and its desires" (43).

So, to become human is the religious task of humankind. Biological nature develops us only up to a certain point, and then we must individually, with great deliberation and with full consciousness, seek the rest. All great scriptures of the world are written in order to provide each of us with a description of this way to become fully human. And herein lies our salvation. As Schuon puts it, "Man is saved by conforming himself perfectly to his theomorphic nature" (104). And conversely, insofar as we are not adequately so conforming ourselves (and again, that is a matter of choice), we are becoming lost.

There is another dimension to Schuon's writing which must be brought forward. It is this: Although we must individually, deliberately and consciously seek to become fully human, Schuon is quick to point out that it is not through our own efforts, ultimately, that we become ourselves. We are not constituted in a way able to bring off our own self-becoming. There is no pulling ourselves up by our own bootstraps. There is no program or method by which we can climb to heaven based solely on our own initiative. That is why all great religions in their basic scriptures stress the radical dependence of the human person upon what in Christianity is called "grace" and what the Chinese call the "energy of Tao." It is that energy which embodies the will of Heaven. If we are to individually fulfill and express our nature, we must first recognize our radical dependence upon that Power which constituted us in the first place. As Schuon tells us, "Nothing can be accomplished without the aid of Heaven" (206). In order to become human, then, one must voluntarily undertake a specific task, a vocation, and perform that task in the continuing recognition that one is dependent for his or her growth upon that Power which constitutes him or her. It is for this reason that the object of becoming human is to become, religiously speaking, divinely human.

Now we come to the raw nerve of it all. If the human person will unconditionally make himself available to the work of that Power we call grace, grace will do the rest. Amazingly, if we devote ourselves entirely and unconditionally which is to say single-mindedly to becoming human, we must on that account become as divinely human; through our devotion, we necessarily participate in the divine life. "[M]an is a point of junction between . . . the outward and the inward: it is precisely in virtue of the dimension of inwardness, which opens onto the Absolute and therefore the infinite, that man is quasi-divine" (41).

Schuon doesn't mean we become God with a capital "G." Rather, insofar as we conform ourselves to our original nature, we participate in the divine life. As we conform ourselves to our original nature, God expresses God's self as us. "The Spirit became flesh that the flesh might become Spirit." And that is why we have in the Church Fathers the statement, "God became man in order that man might become god." And if you write the last "god" with a small "g," you will have precisely what both the Church Fathers and Schuon had in mind.

Schuon ends this book with a beautiful and profound reflection on Saint Bernard's "I love because I love." The deeper meaning of these words, Schuon tells us, points to the fact that "our happiness stems from what we are; we are happy to the extent that we are really and fully ourselves" (220). Just as God is love, we too are love waiting to be realized.

I must add one more thing. It is refreshing that Schuon does not enter into the many elaborate academic debates about religion and the nature of religious experience. He does not argue with the *projectionists* who find the source of religious experience in psychological or sociological forces, nor does he argue with the *constructivists* who view the various religious traditions as culturally constructed responses to a noumenal reality. And rather than encouraging us to remain academically detached, Schuon invites us to take seriously that the life of spirit is the fountain from which our scriptures have come to us, and to take seriously that we too can become explorers, trace the scriptures upstream, drink from the same waters and understand their meaning firsthand through the very source that inspired these scriptures. It is with this in mind that Frithjof Schuon speaks to us in these pages.

Survey of Metaphysics and Esoterism serves as a near complete expression of Schuon's thought. This book is distinctive in presenting, in one volume, what might be called the three hallmarks of Schuon's writings. In clear and distinct order, he writes on cosmology and metaphysical principles, on the esoteric and exoteric expression of these principles in the various religious traditions, and on the trials and ultimate transformation of human nature. And every page is a calling to us, not merely to understand, but to *become* the concrete expression of what we understand.

Fullerton College   Bruce K. Hanson
Fullerton, California   Assistant Professor of
                        Philosophy and Religious Studies

Survey of
Metaphysics
and Esoterism

Preface by the Author

Throughout our works, we have dealt with the perennial religion, explicitly or implicitly, and in connection with the diverse religions which on the one hand veil it and on the other hand allow it to shine through; and we believe we have given a homogeneous and sufficient exposition of this primordial and universal *Sophia*, in spite of our discontinuous and sporadic manner of referring to it. But the *Sophia perennis* is quite evidently inexhaustible and has no natural limits, even in a systematic exposition such as the *Vedānta*. Moreover this systematic quality is neither an advantage nor a disadvantage; depending upon the content it can be one or the other; truth is beautiful in all its forms. In fact, there is no great doctrine that is not a system, and none that expresses itself in an exclusively systematic fashion.

As it is impossible to exhaust all that lends itself to being expressed, and as repetition in metaphysical matters cannot be a mistake — it being better to be too clear than not to be clear enough — we believed we could return to our usual theses, either to offer things we have not yet said, or to explain in a usefully new way things we have said before. If the fundamental data of a doctrine that is abstract by definition are more or less limited by the nature of things — this being the very definition of a system, since the formal elements of a regular crystal cannot be innumerable — the same does not hold true for illustrations or applications, which are without limit and whose function is to grasp

1

better what at first glance does not seem to be sufficiently concrete.

One further remark, this time of a more or less personal order: we grew up at a time when one could still say, without blushing on account of its naivety, that two and two make four; when words still had a meaning and said what they meant to say; when one could conform to the laws of elementary logic or of common sense, without having to pass through psychology or biology, or so-called sociology, and so forth; in short, when there were still points of reference in the intellectual arsenal of men. By this we wish to point out that our way of thinking and our dialectic are deliberately out of date; and we know in advance, for it is only too evident, that the reader to whom we address ourselves will thank us for it.

Introduction: Epistemological Premises

When one speaks of doctrine, one thinks first of all, and rightly so, of an unfolding of concordant concepts; but one must in addition take into account the epistemological aspect of the system in view, and it is this dimension, which also is part of the doctrine, that we wish to examine here by way of introduction.

It is indispensable to know at the outset that there are truths inherent in the human spirit that are as if buried in the "depths of the heart," which means that they are contained as potentialities or virtualities in the pure Intellect: these are the principial and archetypal truths, those which prefigure and determine all others. They are accessible, intuitively and infallibly, to the "gnostic," the "pneumatic," the "theosopher" — in the proper and original meaning of these terms — and they are accessible consequently to the "philosopher" according to the still literal and innocent meaning of the word: to a Pythagoras or a Plato, and to a certain extent even to an Aristotle, in spite of his exteriorizing and virtually scientistic perspective.

And this is of the greatest importance: if there were no pure Intellect — the intuitive and infallible faculty of the immanent Spirit — neither would there be reason, for the miracle of reasoning can be explained and justified only by the miracle of intellection. Animals have no reason because they are incapable of conceiving the Absolute; in

3

other words, if man possesses reason, together with language, it is because he has access in principle to the suprarational vision of the Real and consequently to metaphysical certitude. The intelligence of animals is partial, that of man is total; and this totality is explained only by a transcendent reality to which the intelligence is proportioned.

Thus the decisive error of materialism and of agnosticism is to be blind to the fact that material things and the common experiences of our life are immensely beneath the scope of our intelligence. If the materialists were right, this intelligence would be an inexplicable luxury; without the Absolute, the capacity of conceiving it would have no cause. The truth of the Absolute coincides with the very substance of our spirit; the diverse religions actualize objectively that which is contained in our deepest subjectivity. Revelation is to the macrocosm what intellection is to the microcosm; the Transcendent is immanent in the world, otherwise the world could not exist, and the Immanent is transcendent with respect to the individual, whom otherwise It would not surpass.

What we have just said concerning the scope of human intelligence applies also to the will, in the sense that free will proves the transcendence of its essential goal, for which man has been created and by which man is man; human will is proportioned to God, and it is only in God and by Him that it is totally free. One could say something analogous concerning the human soul: our soul proves God because it is proportioned to the divine Nature, and it is so through compassion, disinterested love, generosity, and therefore, in the final analysis, through objectivity, or the capacity to step outside of our subjectivity and thus to transcend ourselves; this is what characterizes precisely the intelligence and will of man. And it is in these foundations of human nature — image of the divine Nature — that the *religio perennis* is rooted, and with it all religion and all wisdom.

4

To "discern" is to "separate": to separate the Real and the illusory, the Absolute and the contingent, the Necessary and the possible, *Ātmā* and *Māyā*. To discernment is joined, complementally and operatively, "concentration," which "unites": it is — starting from earthly and human *Māyā* — the plenary awareness of *Ātmā* at once absolute, infinite and perfect; without equal, without limit and without blemish. According to certain Church Fathers, "God became man that man might become God": an audacious and elliptical formula which we shall paraphrase in a Vedantic manner by saying that the Real became illusory in order that the illusory might become real; *Ātmā* made Itself *Māyā* in order that *Māyā* might realize *Ātmā*. The Absolute, in Its overflowing fullness, projects contingency and mirrors Itself therein, in a play of reciprocity from which It will emerge as victor, as That which alone is.

*

* *

In the universe there is the known and there is the knower; in *Ātmā*, the two poles are united, the one is inseparably within the other, whereas in *Māyā* this unity is split into subject and object. Depending upon the point of view or the aspect, *Ātmā* is either absolute "Consciousness" — the universal "Witness," the pure "Subject" — or absolute "Being," the "Substance," the pure and transcendent "Object"; It is knowable as "Reality," but It is also the immanent "Knower" of all its own possibilities, first of the hypostatic and then of the existential and existentiated.

And for man, this is of decisive importance: knowledge of the Total demands on man's part totality of knowing. It demands, beyond our thought, all our being, for thought is a part, not the whole; and this indicates the goal of all spiritual life. He who conceives the Absolute — or who believes in God — cannot stop short *de jure* at this knowledge, or at this belief, realized by thought alone; he must

5

on the contrary integrate all that he is into his adherence to the Real, as is demanded precisely by Its absoluteness and infinitude. Man must "become that which he is" because he must "become That which is"; "the soul is all that it knows," said Aristotle.

Moreover, man is not only a thinking being, he is also a willing being, which is to say that totality of intelligence implies freedom of will. This freedom would be meaningless without an end prefigured in the Absolute; without the knowledge of God and of our final ends, it would be neither possible nor useful.

Man is made of thought, of will and of love: he can think truth or error, he can will good or evil, he can love beauty or ugliness.[1] Now thought of the true — or knowledge of the real — demands on the one hand willing of the good and on the other love of the beautiful, hence virtue, for virtue is none other than beauty of soul; that is why the Greeks, who were aesthetes as well as thinkers, included virtue within philosophy. Without beauty of soul, all willing is sterile, it is petty and closes itself to grace; and in an analogous manner: without effort of will, all spiritual thought ultimately remains superficial and ineffectual and leads to pretension. Virtue coincides with a sensibility proportioned — or conformed — to the Truth, and that is why the soul of the sage soars above things and thereby above itself, if one may put it thus; whence the disinterestedness, nobleness and generosity of great souls.

---

1. A nuance is perhaps needed here, in spite of its evidentness: one loves a man of good will even if he is ugly, but it is obviously because of his inner beauty; and this beauty is immortal whereas outward ugliness is transitory. Nevertheless it must not be forgotten that outward beauty, even when combined with an inner ugliness, testifies to beauty as such, which is of a celestial nature and must not be scorned in any of its manifestations. The calumny of physical beauty by many ascetics can be useful in regard to human weakness, but it is nonetheless inadequate and impious from a more profound point of view.

Quite clearly, the consciousness of metaphysical principles cannot go hand in hand with moral pettiness, such as ambition and hypocrisy: "Be ye perfect even as your Father in Heaven is perfect."

There is something that man must know and think; and something that he must will and do; and something that he must love and be. He must know that God is necessary Being, which therefore suffices unto Itself; that It is that which cannot not be, whereas the world is merely the possible, which may or may not be; all other distinctions and valuations derive from this fundamental distinction. In addition, man must will what brings him closer to God directly or indirectly; the chief content of this willing being prayer, the response given to God, and which includes metaphysical meditation as well as mystical concentration. Finally, man must love "in God" that which testifies to the divine Beauty, and more generally all that is conformed to the Nature of God; he must love the Good, that is to say the Norm, in all its possible forms; and since the Norm necessarily transcends the limitations of the ego, man must tend towards transcending his own limits. It is necessary to love the Norm or the Archetype more than its reflections, hence more than the contingent ego; and it is this self-knowledge and this disinterested love which constitute all nobleness of soul.

*

* *

There is a question that has always been raised, rightly or wrongly: are metaphysical realities necessarily explainable, or at least, are there not mysterious situations that can be expressed only by paradox, or even by the absurd? All too often this argument has been used in order to mask flaws in theological doctrines, whose subjective imperfections have been objectified: since one is not able to resolve given enigmas, one decrees that the "human mind" is incapable of doing so, and the blame is laid primarily on logic, "Aristotelian" or other, as if logic were synonymous with rationalism, doubt and ignorance.

On the plane of natural things it suffices to have at one's disposal the necessary data and then to reason correctly; the same conditions apply on the plane of supernatural things, with the difference that the object of thought then requires the intervention of intellection, which is an inner illumination; for if natural things may require a certain intuition independent of reasoning as such, then supernatural things will *a fortiori* require intuition of a superior order, since they do not fall within reach of the senses. As we have said more than once, reason requires data in order to function, otherwise it operates in the void: these data are furnished, firstly by the world, which as such is objective; secondly, and in combination with the preceding factor, by experience, which as such is subjective; thirdly, by Revelation, which like the world is objective since it comes to us from without; fourthly, by intellection, which is subjective since it is produced within ourselves.

One thing leading to another, we believe we have the right to insert here the following remark: as with all relativism, existentialism contradicts itself; imagining itself to be the great adversary of rationalism, it wishes to put experience in place of reasoning, without in the least wondering why reasoning exists, or how experience can be extolled without having recourse to reason. It is precisely experience itself which demonstrates that reasoning is something effectual, otherwise no one would reason; and it is the very existence of reason which shows that this faculty must have an object. Animals undergo many experiences, but they do not reason; whereas on the contrary man can avoid many experiences by reasoning. To wish to replace reasoning by experience on the practical plane and in a relative fashion could still be meaningful; but to do so on the intellectual and speculative plane, as the empiricists and existentialists wish to do, is properly speaking demented. For the inferior man, only what is contingent is real, and he seeks by his method to lower principles to the level of contingencies when he does not deny them purely and simply. This mentality of the *shūdra* has infiltrated Christian theology and has committed its well-known ravages.[2]

But let us return, after this parenthesis, to the problems of spiritual epistemology. No doubt, logic has limits, but it is the first to support this observation, otherwise it would not be logical, precisely; however, the limits of logic depend upon the nature of things and not upon a confessional edict. The limitlessness of space and time seems absurd in that logic cannot express it in a concrete and exhaustive fashion; it is perfectly logical however to notice that this double limitlessness exists. And no logic forbids us to know with certitude that this phenomenon results from the principial Infinite, a mystery that our thought cannot explore and which is manifested precisely through spatial unfolding and temporal transformation, or again by the limitlessness of number. In an analogous manner, the empirical uniqueness of the ego — the fact of being such and such an ego and not some other, and of being the only one that is "itself" — this uniqueness cannot be explained concretely by logic, and yet logic is perfectly capable of expressing it in an abstract manner, with the aid of the principles of the necessary and the possible, and thus of escaping the pitfall of absurdity.[3]

2. Some modernist theologians readily admit that there is a God — they find a few reasons for doing so — but they wish to justify this in a "provisional" and not in a "fixed" manner, while refusing of course the definitive formulations of the scholastics; whereas on this plane the truth is either definitive or it is not. A mode of knowledge which is incapable of furnishing the truth to us now, will never furnish it.

3. Subjectivity as such participates in necessary Being because the Absolute is pure Consciousness; the relativity — and thus the manifestation and diversity — of subjectivity is also necessary by virtue of the divine Radiation, which results from the Infinite. This is to say that a

Unquestionably, the Sacred Scriptures contain contradictions; the traditional commentaries take them into account, not by contesting the right of logic to notice them and to satisfy our needs for logical explanations, but by seeking out the underlying link which abolishes the apparent absurdity, the latter being in reality an ellipsis.

If the wisdom of Christ is "folly in the eyes of the world," it is because the "world" is opposed to the "kingdom of God which is within you," and for no other reason; it is certainly not because it claims for itself a mysterious right to what is nonsensical, *quod absit*.[4] The wisdom of Christ is "folly" because it does not flatter the exteriorizing perversion, both dispersing and hardening, which characterizes the man of concupiscence, sin and error; it is this perversion which precisely constitutes the "world"; this perversion with its insatiable scientific and philosophical curiosity which perpetuates the sin of Eve and Adam and repeats it in indefinitely diverse forms.[5]

particular subjectivity is a possibility; its principle pertains to the Absolute; and its particularity pertains to relativity or contingency. But it would be absurd to ask why it is "I" who am "I," and logic does not suffer thereby in the least.

4. Let us mention by way of example the following contradiction: according to the Bible, God raised Enoch up to Him, and Elias mounted up to Heaven in a chariot of fire; but according to the Catholic creed, Christ "descended into hell" in order to take to Heaven all men who had lived before him, including Enoch and Elias, who at that time were also "below" whereas God had placed them "above." All this in order to say that no one is saved except by the divine Logos; but as this Logos is in reality intemporal, it acts independently of history, which of course does not prevent It from manifesting Itself in human form, hence in history. Let us note in this connection that the Church Fathers, in speaking of the "bosom of Abraham," have prudently added: "whatever may be understood by this word."

5. It is very strange that the Church discerns this perversion only on the dogmatic and moral planes; this blindness has something providential about it in the sense that "it must needs be that offenses come."

10

On the plane of religious controversies, to claim a monopoly for illogicality and to attribute a Luciferian fault to the elementary logic of the contradictor, all in the name of a so-called translogical, but in fact objectively unverifiable, "pneumatology" — this claim, we say, is obviously unacceptable, for it is merely an obscurantist monologue and at the same time a double-edged sword by its very subjectivism; all dialogue becomes impossible, which moreover excuses the interlocutor from converting, for man owes nothing to a message that claims to divest itself of the laws of human thought. On the other hand, the mere fact of subjective experience never offers a valid doctrinal argument; if experience is correct, it can always express itself in a satisfactory or at least sufficient manner.[6]

Metaphysical Truth is both expressible and inexpressible: inexpressible, it is not however unknowable, for the Intellect opens onto the Divine Order and therefore encompasses all that is; and expressible, it becomes crystallized in formulations which are all they ought to be since they communicate all that is necessary or useful to our mind. Forms are doors to the essences, in thought and in language as well as in all other symbolisms.

---

6. We speak here of doctrine, hence conceptualization, not mystery. It goes without saying that not all mystical experience can be translated into words, but no true mystic would dream of turning a simple experience into a specifically doctrinal argument; otherwise doctrines would be pointless, and so would language.

11

Part One

The World of Principles

Summary of Integral Metaphysics

In metaphysics, it is necessary to start from the idea that the Supreme Reality is absolute, and that being absolute it is infinite. That is absolute which allows of no augmentation or diminution, or of no repetition or division; it is therefore that which is at once solely itself and totally itself. And that is infinite which is not determined by any limiting factor and therefore does not end at any boundary; it is in the first place Potentiality or Possibility as such, and *ipso facto* the Possibility of things, hence Virtuality. Without All-Possibility, there would be neither Creator nor creation, neither *Māyā* nor *Samsāra*.

The Infinite is so to speak the intrinsic dimension of plenitude proper to the Absolute; to say Absolute is to say Infinite, the one being inconceivable without the other. We can symbolize the relation between these two aspects of Supreme Reality by the following images: in space, the absolute is the point, and the infinite is extension; in time, the absolute is the moment, and the infinite is duration. On the plane of matter, the absolute is the ether — the underlying and omnipresent primordial substance — whereas the infinite is the indefinite series of substances; on the plane of form, the absolute is the sphere — the simple, perfect and primordial form — and the infinite is the indefinite series of more or less complex forms; finally, on the plane of number, the absolute will be unity or unicity, and the infinite will be the unlimited series of numbers or possible quantities, or totality.

15

The distinction between the Absolute and the Infinite expresses the two fundamental aspects of the Real, that of essentiality and that of potentiality; this is the highest principial prefiguration of the masculine and feminine poles. Universal Radiation, thus *Māyā* both divine and cosmic, springs from the second aspect, the Infinite, which coincides with All-Possibility.

*

* *

The "Sovereign Good" is the First Cause inasmuch as it is revealed by phenomena that we term "good," precisely, which is to say that the real and the good coincide. Indeed, it is positive phenomena that attest to the Supreme Reality, and not negative, privative or subversive phenomena; the latter would manifest nothingness, "if it existed," and do so in a certain indirect and paradoxical respect, in the sense that nothingness corresponds to an end that is unrealizable but nonetheless tends towards realization. Evil is the "possibility of the impossible," lacking which the Infinite would not be the Infinite; to ask why All-Possibility includes the possibility of its own negation — a possibility always reinitiated but never fully actualized — is like asking why Existence is Existence, or why Being is Being.

Therefore, if we call the Supreme Principle the Good, *Agathón,* or if we say it is the Sovereign Good that is the Absolute and hence the Infinite, it is not because we paradoxically limit the Real, but because we know that every good stems from it and manifests it essentially, and thus reveals its Nature. Assuredly it can be said that the Divinity is "beyond good and evil," but on condition of adding that this "beyond" is in its turn a "good" in the sense that it testifies to an Essence in which there could be no shadow of limitation or privation, and which consequently cannot but be the absolute Good or absolute Plenitude; all of which is perhaps difficult to explain, but not impossible to conceive.

16

The diverse manifestations of the Good in the world clearly have their source in a principial and archetypal diversity, whose root is situated in the Supreme Principle itself, and which pertains not only to the Divine Qualities, from which our virtues are derived, but also — in another respect — to aspects of the Divine Personality, from which our faculties are derived; we shall speak of this again below.

Still in connection with the reverberations of the aspects or modes of the Sovereign Good, we also have to consider the relationships of Transcendence and Immanence, the first being connected more to the aspect of Absoluteness, and the second to that of Infinitude. According to the first relationship, God alone is the Good; He alone possesses, for example, the quality of beauty; compared to the divine Beauty, the beauty of a creature is nothing, just as existence itself is nothing next to Divine Being; all this from the point of view of Transcendence. The perspective of Immanence also starts from the axiom that God alone possesses both the qualities and reality; but its conclusion is positive and participative, and thus it will be said that the beauty of a creature — being beauty and not its contrary — is necessarily that of God, since there is no other; and the same is true for all the other qualities, without forgetting, at their basis, the miracle of existence. The perspective of Immanence does not nullify creaturely qualities, as does that of Transcendence, but on the contrary makes them divine, if one may so express it.

*

* *

All our preceding considerations evoke the question of the "why" of universal Manifestation and, secondarily, as a result of this question, the problem of evil. To answer the question of why there is a relativity, hence a *Māyā*, and consequently a Manifestation, we may refer in the first place to an idea of Saint Augustine which we have men-

17

tioned more than once, namely that it is in the nature of the Good to wish to communicate itself: to say Good is to say radiation, projection, unfolding, gift of self. But at the same time, to say radiation is to say distance, hence alienation or impoverishment; the solar rays dim and become lost in the night of space. From this arises, at the end of the trajectory, the paradoxical phenomenon of evil, which nonetheless has the positive function of highlighting the good *a contrario,* and of contributing in its fashion to equilibrium in the phenomenal order.

A remark concerning the divergence between the Aryan or Greco-Hindu idea of "universal Manifestation" and the Semitic or monotheistic idea of "Creation" is called for here. The first idea refers to the world inasmuch as it results from an ontological necessity, that of radiation or of communication of the good, precisely; in other words, *Māyā* springs from the Infinitude of the Supreme Principle; and to say *Māyā* is to say *samsāra,* the world of "transmigration." As for the Semitic idea of Creation, it refers to the world, considered not in its totality, but reduced to a single cycle and conceived as the effect of a single "free" act of God. In reality, the creation to which we belong is but one cycle of universal manifestation, this manifestation being composed of an indefinite number of cycles that are "necessary" as regards their existence but "free" as regards their particularity. The Universe is a fabric woven of necessity and freedom, of mathematical rigor and musical play; every phenomenon participates in these two principles.

*

* *

The first distinction to be made in a complete doctrine is that between the Absolute and the relative, or between the Infinite and the finite; between *Ātmā* and *Māyā.* The first term expresses a priori the single Essence, the

18

Eckhartian "Godhead" (*Gottheit*), Beyond-Being; the "personal God" already pertains to *Māyā*, of which He is the "relatively absolute" summit; He encompasses the entire domain of relativity down to the extreme limit of the cosmogonic projection.

The second "qualitative" and "descending" distinction to be made is that between the Principle and Manifestation, God and the world. The Principle includes the Absolute and its reflection within relativity, namely Being or the personal God, precisely; the distinction here is that between the "pure Absolute" and the "relative Absolute", the latter being relative in relation to the Absolute as such, but absolute in relation to the world. As for Manifestation, it extends from the central reflection of the Principle — the Logos, the celestial, angelic and avataric world — to the peripheral, infra-celestial, purely "natural" and samsaric world.

A third distinction-synthesis to be made is that between "Heaven" and "earth," the latter word having to be taken in a symbolic or analogical sense: the celestial order includes on the one hand the two "degrees" of the Principle itself, namely the "pure Absolute" and the Absolute colored by relativity, and on the other hand the Principle manifested at the center of the cosmos, namely the Logos; whereas the "earthly" order — whether it is a question of our earth or of other analogous worlds that necessarily remain unknown to us — is this purely "natural" world that we have mentioned above.

A fourth fundamental distinction situates the Logos at the center: on the one hand it is situated below the pure Absolute and above the "natural" and "profane" world, and on the other hand it combines the "celestial" and the "earthly" — or the "divine" and the "human" — owing to the fact that it includes the already relative dimension of the Principle as well as the manifestation of this Principle at the cosmic center. The Logos is the "uncreated Word"; it is "true man and true God."

All of this means that the total Universe comprises four fundamental degrees: the Principle as such, which is the "pure Absolute"; the Principle already included in *Māyā*, which is God the Creator, Legislator and Savior; the Principle reflected in the created order, which is the "celestial" order, and also the *Avatāra;* and the peripheral creation, which is purely "horizontal" and "natural." In other words: firstly, the Principle in itself; secondly, the prefiguration of Manifestation in the Principle; thirdly, the projection of the Principle in Manifestation; and fourthly, Manifestation in itself. This is to say that the line of demarcation changes place or level according to the perspective.

*

* *

The relation between the Absolute and the relative — between *Ātmā* and *Māyā* — implies three situations or tendencies: firstly, conformity to the Principle, or the "upward" tendency; secondly, the expansive affirmation of possibilities, hence "horizontal" — or, if one prefers, "passional" — existence; and thirdly, non-conformity to the Principle, and thus the "downward" tendency, the illusory movement in the direction of a "nothingness" that is inexistent, obviously, but that is possible as a negative and subversive point of reference. These are the three *gunas* of the Hindu doctrine, which penetrate and regulate all that is created.

But there is not only this hierarchy of situations or tendencies, there is also in the Universe the diversifying manifestation of the positive possibilities included in the divine Potentiality: thus there is the complementarity between the active and passive functions, the masculine and feminine poles, as well as the faculties and qualities that we encounter everywhere in the world and that we ourselves possess to one degree or another. All the cosmic possibilities derive from these principles and their indefinitely diverse combinations.

To be more explicit, we will say: there is first of all, on "this" side of the one Substance — and in a sense as a reflection of the aspects "Absolute" and "Infinite" — the duality of the creative functions, or of the masculine and feminine poles. This is the duality "Activity-Passivity" from which are derived all the analogous functions at all levels of the Universe. Next, and again at all the universal levels — including the divine summit of *Māyā* — there is the trinity of the divine and universal faculties: "Consciousness-Power-Love"; all the capacities of knowing, willing and loving derive from this trinity. After this trinity, in this series of numerical conceptualizations, comes the quaternity of the fundamental qualities, namely "Purity" or "Rigor," "Life" or "Gentleness," "Strength" or "Act," and "Beauty" or "Goodness" or "Peace" or "Beatitude"; these are, analogically, the quaternity "Cold-Heat-Dryness-Humidity," to which moreover correspond the cardinal points.

As we have seen, the trinity includes the faculties that are at once divine and creaturely: the capacities to know, to will and to love. In the medieval Masonic ternary "Wisdom-Strength-Beauty," these faculties are expressed by their qualitative aspects: Wisdom is the content of knowledge; Strength is the virtue of will; Beauty is the ideal object of love. In the Vedantic trinity "Being-Consciousness-Bliss," the faculties are reduced to their ontological essences; in a certain sense they are the ternary "Object-Subject-Union," the first element evoking will, the second, knowledge, and the third, love; the pole "Being," *Sat*, potentially contains "Power," whence its connection with will.[1] Another Hindu Trinity — less fundamental than the

---

1. Let us note at this juncture that the Trinity which the Koran attributes to Christianity — the Father, the Son, the Virgin — is altogether logical in its way and corresponds to what we have just expounded; as for the Christian Trinity proper, the Holy Ghost, like the Virgin, represents the mystery of Divine Love.

preceding — is the *Trimūrti,* the "Triple Manifestation": on the one hand, it is put in relation with the three cosmic tendencies — the ascending, the expansive and the descending — in which case it represents a hierarchy or a "verticality"; on the other hand, and more directly, it pertains to the point of view of "horizontality," since it represents a system of quasi-equivalent and complementary terms. *Shiva* is comparable to the dark and descending tendency inasmuch as he negates and destroys; but he also pertains to the divine aspect *Chit,* "Consciousness" — or "Knowledge" — inasmuch as he reduces to ashes the "Great Illusion," *Mahā-Moha,* and this represents an intrinsically positive function.

Let us summarize: the principial numbers — or the numerical symbols — are either "horizontal" or "vertical," according to whether they indicate either a differentiation, which is reflected at every universal level, or a projection, which penetrates into relativity. When the duality is horizontal, it expresses the "active" and "passive" poles; when it is vertical, it expresses the "absolute" and "relative" degrees, firstly in the Divine Order, and then in the cosmic order. When the trinity is horizontal it expresses the faculties, which a priori are divine; when it is vertical, it expresses the cosmic tendencies. Finally, when the quaternity is horizontal, it refers to the universal qualities; when it is vertical, it indicates the degrees of the Universe — the penetration into relativity — as described above.

Perfection and Projection; the whole structure of the Universe is expressed by these two words. The "horizontal" numbers relate to the polarizations of the Divine Perfection, and the "vertical" numbers to the degrees of the cosmogonic Projection.

Here a specification is called for regarding the aspects of the Sovereign Good: there is no need to consider a trinity formed by the aspects "Good," "Absolute," "Infinite"; but rather, what ought to be said is that the Sovereign

Good is absolute and, therefore, that it is infinite. The Divine Good, by its very nature, "wills to communicate itself" or "to radiate," and this "will" is necessarily prefigured, if one may say so, in its intrinsic nature.

*

* *

According to a German proverb, "He who says A must say B" *(Wer A sagt, muss B sagen)*, and this applies also, and even above all, to knowledge. The unicity of the Divine Object requires the totality of the human subject; this is the principle and the key of Sacred Doctrine, and it is what distinguishes it from profane philosophy, which may ask man to inflate himself, but will never ask him to surpass himself.

The total exigency of Sacred Doctrine — of "theosophy" in the proper sense of the word — results from the fact that the human intelligence is by definition capable of objectivity and transcendence and implies *ipso facto* the same capacity for the will and for the feeling soul; whence the freedom of our will and the moral instinct of our soul. And just as our intelligence is fully human only through truths concerning God and our last ends, so too is our will fully human only through its operative participation in these truths; and similarly, our soul is human only by its morality, its detachment and its magnanimity, hence by its love of the Truth and the Way. To say that free will and moral sensibility are part of the intelligence of *homo sapiens*, means that there is no consequential and plenary metaphysical knowledge without the participation of these two faculties, the volitive and the affective; to know completely is to be. The circle of knowledge closes in our personality, in its death in God and in its life in God. And "where your treasure is, there will your heart be also."

Dimensions, Modes and Degrees
of the Divine Order

The idea that the Supreme Principle is both absolute
Reality and thus infinite Possibility, can suffice unto itself,
for it contains everything, in particular the necessity of a
universal Manifestation. From a less synthetic point of
view however, and one closer to *Māyā*, we may consider a
third hypostatic element, namely perfect Quality; being
the Absolute, the Principle is thereby the Infinite and the
Perfect. Absoluteness of the Real, infinitude of the Possible, perfection of the Good; these are the "initial dimensions" of the Divine Order.

This Order also comprises "modes": Wisdom, Power,
Goodness; that is, the content or the substance of the Supreme Principle consists in these three modes and each of
them is at once absolute, infinite and perfect; for each divine mode participates by definition in the nature of the
divine Substance and thus comprises absolute Reality, infinite Possibility and perfect Quality. In Wisdom, as in
Power and in Goodness, there is no contingency, no limitation and no imperfection: being absolute, these modes
cannot not be; being infinite, they are inexhaustible; being
perfect, they lack nothing.

The Principle not only possesses "dimensions" and
"modes," it also has "degrees," by virtue of its very Infinitude which projects the Principles into Relativity and
thereby produces, so to speak, the metacosmic "space"

that we term the Divine Order. These degrees are the divine Essence, the divine Potentiality and the divine Manifestation; or Beyond-Being, creative Being, and the Spirit or the existentiating Logos which constitutes the divine Center of the total cosmos.

Necessity and Liberty; Unicity and Totality.[1] On the one hand, the Absolute is "necessary" Being, that which must be, which cannot not be, and which for that very reason is unique; on the other hand, the Infinite is "free" Being, which is limitless and which contains all that can be, and which for that very reason is total.

This Reality, absolute and infinite, necessary and free, unique and total, is *ipso facto* perfect: for it lacks nothing, and it possesses in consequence all that is positive; it suffices unto itself. This means that the Absolute, as well as the Infinite which is as it were its intrinsic complement or its *shakti,* coincides with Perfection; the Sovereign Good is the very substance of the Absolute.

In the world, the existence of things, hence their relative reality, is derived from the Absolute; their containers, their diversity and their multiplicity, thus space, time, form, number, are derived from the Infinite; and finally, their qualities, whether substantial or accidental, are derived from Perfection. For Perfection, the Sovereign Good, contains the three modes or hypostatic functions which we have mentioned, namely: Intelligence or Consciousness, or Wisdom, or Ipseity; Power or Strength; and Goodness, which coincides with Beauty and Beatitude. It is Infinitude which so to speak projects the Sovereign Good into relativity, or in other words, which creates relativity, *Māyā;* it is in relativity that the supreme Qualities become differentiated and give rise to the Qualities of

1. Even in the natural order, a thing that is positively or qualitatively unique is always total; perfect beauty cannot be poor, it is by definition a synthesis, whence its aspects of limitlessness and appeasement.

26

the creating, inspiring and acting Divinity, thus to the personal God; it is from Him that all the cosmic qualities with their indefinite gradations and differentiations are derived.

To say Absolute is to say Reality and Sovereign Good; to say Infinite is to say in addition communication, radiation, and in consequence, relativity; hence also differentiation, contrast, privation; the Infinite is All-Possibility. *Ātmā* wills to clothe even nothingness, and it does so by and in *Māyā*.[2]

It is necessary to distinguish between the Good in itself and the manifestations of the Good: the Good in itself has no opposite; but once it is reflected in the manifested order, which is the cosmic order, it appears in the form of a given good, and this particularism necessarily implies the possibility of a given evil; relative good can be produced only in a world of contrasts.

To say, out of a concern for transcendence, that the Absolute is "beyond good and evil, beauty and ugliness," can only mean one thing, namely that It is the Good in itself, Beauty in itself; it cannot mean that It is deprived of goodness or beauty. Moreover, if on the one hand the possibility of the manifestation of a good necessarily makes the manifestation of evil possible, on the other hand every manifested good, being limited by definition, implies the possibility of another manifested good; God alone is unique, because He alone remains outside of manifestation.

The fragmentariness, as it were, of manifested goods appears in an eloquent manner in sexual love or more precisely in the natural selection which it implies: a given limited good — a given individual viewed in respect of his qualities — wishes to complete himself by another given limited but complementary good, thus to create a new be-

---

2. Principially and analogically speaking, *Māyā* is not only "spatial," it is also "temporal": there are not only extension and hierarchy, there are also change and rhythm; there are worlds and cycles.

ing in whom the fragments are united. This new being is limited in his turn, of course, since he is still comprised within manifestation; but he is less limited from the standpoint of a given intention of natural selection, and less limited from the standpoint of love, which tends to transcend individuals — intrinsically by its spiritual magic, and extrinsically by the unitive creation of a new being. It is thus that man is in search of himself, of his totality and his deiformity; and in seeking himself, he seeks God, unconsciously or consciously: either binding or liberating himself.

*

* *

In the Absolute there is no differentiation, for the latter by definition pertains to relativity, to *Māyā;* if it be objected that the Infinite and the Good — or Infinitude and Perfection — pertain to the Absolute, our reply is that the separation of these aspects or dimensions is subjective, it is in our mind, whereas in the Absolute these same aspects are undifferentiated while remaining real in respect of their intrinsic nature.

In the Essence — in the "pure Absolute" — Intelligence, Power and Goodness are likewise situated within and not alongside one another;[3] so that we can say that the Absolute — or the Absolute-Infinite-Good — is Intelligence, or that it is Power, or that it is Goodness, in their intrinsic and purely principial reality. In relation to Intelli-

---

3. If one refers to the Vedantic ternary *Sat* ("pure Being"), *Chit* ("Consciousness"), *Ānanda* ("Beatitude"), it is necessary to bear in mind that the aspect "Power" derives from the aspect "pure Being." In physics, it will be said that "energy" is bound up with "mass"; the proof of this is that magnetism in celestial bodies is proportional to their size or density.

gence, it will be said that the Absolute is the Self, which is expressed by the term *Ātmā;* thus viewed, the Absolute is the Subject as such, the real and only Subject; extrinsically and combined with *Māyā,* this Subject will be the root of all possible subjectivities, it will be the immanent "divine I." In relation to Power, it will be said that the Absolute is the "absolutely Other," the Transcendent as well as the principial Omnipotent; extrinsically and combined with *Māyā,* it will be the underlying Agent of all acts as such, but not inasmuch as they are intentions and forms.[4] Finally, in relation to Goodness or Beauty, it will be said that the Absolute coincides with supreme Beatitude, and that extrinsically and combined with *Māyā,* it will be the generous "Father," but also the merciful "Mother": infinitely blissful in itself, it gives existence as well as the goods of existence; it offers all that it is in its Essence.

The Infinite, by its radiation brought about so to speak by the pressure — or the overflowing — of the innumerable possibilities, transposes the substance of the Absolute, namely the Sovereign Good, into relativity; this transposition gives rise a priori to the reflected image of the Good, namely creative Being. The Good, which coincides with the Absolute, is thus prolonged in the direction of relativity and first gives rise to Being which contains the archetypes, and then to Existence which manifests them in indefinitely varied modes and according to the rhythms of the diverse cosmic cycles.

The Absolute is that which "cannot not be"; and the necessity of Being excludes all "that is not It." In an analogous but as it were inverse manner, the Infinite is that which "can be all"; and the liberty of Being includes "all

---

4. It is here that is situated the Asharite theory of the human "acquisition" *(kasb)* of the divine Acts: it is God alone who acts, since He alone is capable of it; it is He who "creates" our acts, but it is we who "acquire" them *(naksibūn).*

29

that is It"; hence all that is possible, this "all" being limitless, precisely. In other words: God alone is necessary Being: in Him there is nothing contingent or, for all the more reason, arbitrary; on the contrary, outside of Him there are only contingent existences. And God alone is free Being: in Him there is no determination *ab extra* or any constraint, and on the contrary, outside of Him, there are only the existences that He determines. On the one hand, an existence may or may not be, and that is its contingency; on the other hand, the existence of a thing contains one possibility only, that of that thing and nothing else, and that is its limitation; whereas the Being of God contains all that is possible.

Or again: by His nature, hence by necessity, God "must" create; but He "is free" to create what He wills by virtue of His liberty; creation itself is "necessary," but God is free as regards the modalities. In other words: God "is free" to create what He wills — and He can will only in conformity with His Nature — but He "must" follow the logic of things; His "activity" in laws and structures is necessary, while in its contents it is free.

*

*   *

Existence is subject to Being, but Being in its turn is subject or subordinate to Beyond-Being; in other words, the world is subject to God, but God in His turn is subject to His own Essence: to the "pure Absolute," to *Ātmā* without trace of *Māyā*. God can do anything in the world; but He can do nothing except what His Essence or His Nature "dictates," and He can will nothing else. God cannot be what He "wills," except in the sense that He wills only what He is; now He is the Sovereign Good.

Certainly, God the Creator is the absolute Master of the created world; but *Ātmā* is the absolute Master of *Māyā*, and the Creator pertains to *Māyā* since within it, He is the direct and central reflection of *Ātmā*.

30

That Beyond-Being can have "on its level" — if provisionally one may express oneself thus — a will other than that which Being has on its own level, is no more contradictory than the fact that a given aspect of Being, or a given "Divine Name," can have a will different from that of another given aspect of Being. The "Generous" for example, can or must will something other than what is willed by the "Avenger"; the "vertical" diversity in the Divine Order is no more contrary to Unity than is the "horizontal" diversity. That God as Legislator does not will sin whereas God as All-Possibility wills it — but from an altogether different point of view of course — is as plausible as the fact that the Divine Justice has aims other than those of the Divine Mercy.[5]

"God doeth what He wills": quite paradoxically, it is just this and analogous Koranic expressions[6] which indicate absolute Transcendence and which refer — in the language of creating and revealing Being — to the unfathomable Beyond-Being, hence to the transpersonal Essence of the Divinity. The very paradox of the expression, which eludes all explanation, all logical and moral satisfaction, insinuates a reality that transcends the domain of the personal Divine Subject; the apparent arbitrariness here opens the way to metaphysical clarification. In reality, the elusiveness of the phrasing is a key to profundity; the function of the words here is the reverse of the interpretations — tending towards rather coarse exaggerations — of the Hanbalite, Asharite and other theologians. "God doeth what He wills" means, in the final analysis, "God is not what ye think," or rather: "what ye can understand," namely an anthropomorphic being having a single subjectivity and thereby a single will.

---

5. This is well understood by the "polytheists."
6. There are notably the allusions to what is "hidden" *(ghayb)*, and sayings like this one: "God knoweth and ye know not."

God can will what He is, He cannot be what He wills, assuming — with regard to the second proposition — that He could will no matter what, which is precisely what His Being excludes. The following remark is called for here: in a certain respect, God is the absolute Good; but in another respect, He is "beyond good and evil," depending upon the interpretation of the words, as we have noted above. On the one hand, He is the Good in the sense that He is necessarily the cause of all that exists, since there is no other cause in the universe; and existence in itself is neither good nor bad, even though it can be viewed in terms of both aspects. Compared to the "Sovereign Good," the whole world can appear as a kind of "evil" since it is not God — "Why callest thou me good?" — whereas in another respect, "God saw that it was good," that is, the world is good as divine Manifestation; and this shows clearly that, if on the one hand God is "the Good," on the other hand He is "beyond good and evil":[7] in the latter respect — and in that one only — it can be said that the distinction in question means nothing to God, and that consequently human morality does not concern Him.

The Divine Order is made of Wisdom, Power and Goodness, each of these Hypostases being absolute, infinite and perfect. In addition, this Order comprises three degrees of Reality, namely Beyond-Being, Being and Existence: the latter is here, not cosmic Existence as a whole, but the Divine Manifestation, namely the direct and central reflection of Being in the cosmic order;[8] it is thus that

---

7. It should be noted that, if the Koran did not specify that it is God who "created evil" *(min sharri mā khalaq),* the door would remain open for a Mazdean or Manichean dualism: one would risk admitting two divinities, one good and one evil. The Koranic solution is situated so to speak between two pitfalls: the idea of two antagonistic gods, and the pure and simple negation of evil; the Arab or Near-Eastern collective mentality does not seem to have left any other choice.

8. This "Divine Manifestation" is none other than the *Buddhi* of the Vedantists, or the archangelic domain of the Monotheists.

32

the Divine Order enters into the cosmos without ceasing to be what it is, and without the cosmos ceasing to be what it is. And this is also the mystery of the Logos, of the *Avatāra:* of the human theophany that is "true man and true God."

The polarization into distinct Qualities starts at the degree of "Being" and becomes more marked from the degree of "Existence" onwards. Among the Divine Qualities, those which manifest Rigor, Justice, Wrath, derive specifically and in the final analysis from the pole "Absolute" which is not a pole in itself but which appears to be once its *shakti*, Infinitude, is viewed separately. Correlatively and complementally, the Qualities that manifest Gentleness, Compassion, Love, derive in an analogous manner from the pole "Infinite"; this is the Islamic distinction between "Majesty" *(Jalāl)* and "Beauty" *(Jamāl)*. But the "Just" and the "Merciful" are both the "Holy"; for God is One and He is holy by virtue of His Essence, not by virtue of a given Quality.

Justice, or Rigor, deriving as it does from the pole "Absolute," cannot not be; thus in the cosmos there must be supports that permit its manifestation. Likewise for Clemency, or Gentleness, which derives from the pole "Infinite": it can manifest itself only through created elements which serve as receptacles for its action. This evokes the Pauline doctrine of the vessels of Wrath and the vessels of Mercy, hence the idea of predestination; the latter being none other than the substance of a given existential possibility.

All-Possibility, whatever its hypostatic level,[9] prefigures, in its limitlessness both static and dynamic, the comple-

---

9. Beyond-Being, Being or Existence; in other words, whether the pure Infinite *(Ānanda)*, or its prolongation in Being *(= Prakṛti)*, or the limitlessness of the existentiating cosmic Substance *(= Saraswatī-Lakshmī-Parvatī)*. According to Paracelsus, God "the Son" presupposes, not only "the Father," but also "the Mother"; the latter is more or less

33

mentarity "space-time," or more concretely the complementarity of the ether and its vibratory power; the ether
being, in our material world, the basic substance which
prefigures in its turn the complementarity "mass-energy."
And let us recall at this point that the spatial void is in reality the ether, that it is consequently a relative and symbolic
void; likewise, the temporal void, so to speak — the absence of change or movement — is in reality the latent
energy of the etheric element, for there is no absolute inertia. Concrete space is a substance, or the Substance, the
first of all substances; and this substance is a vibration, or
the Vibration, the one which is the vehicle of all the others.
If empirical emptiness were absolute as only a principle
can be, it would be a pure nothingness, and no extension
— temporal or spatial — would be possible, for a nothingness cannot be added to another nothingness; the point
then could not concretely engender the line, or the moment, time. Only a substance — by definition energetic or
vibratory — can vehicle contents, either static or dynamic.

Certainly, space as mere container is empty and life-
less — although it realizes this aspect only in a relative and
fragmentary fashion — but as the field of manifestation
of formal possibilities, and thus in its integral nature, it is
plenitude and movement; and that is why there is in fact
no total space without celestial bodies, and there are no
celestial bodies without change and displacement. If space
were only an emptiness devoid of substantiality and energy, and containing forms by miracle, it would be merely

hidden in the "Father," and it is Mary who embodies her on the human
plane. This opinion is plausible in the sense that the Infinite can be
considered metaphorically — if we accept this kind of symbolism and
assuming a framework that makes it possible — as the "Spouse" *(Shakti)*
of the Absolute and the "Mother" of the Divine Perfection or of the Supreme Good; the Infinite will then be necessarily reflected, in a direct
manner, in the Woman-*Avatāra.*

a museum of crystals; we say "by miracle," for an absolute void, being nothing, can contain nothing.

This is necessarily so, because divine Possibility, while being a void in relation to Manifestation, is in itself Plenitude and Life.[10]

10. In rationalism, it will be said that All-Possibility is an abstraction, whereas in reality it is a potentiality, or Potentiality as such. We would add that All-Possibility is not only a divine "dimension," it is also total *Māyā*, from Being down to our world.

Substance: Subject and Object

Since the Divine Substance, in virtue of one of its dimensions, "willed" and "had to" manifest the world with its multiplicity, it willed and had to manifest at the same time witnesses to this world and this multiplicity, otherwise the Universe would be like an unknown space filled with blind stones, and not a world perceived in accordance with a multitude of aspects. Where there are objects, there must also be subjects: creatures which are the witnesses of things belong indissolubly to creation. In its unfolding, the veil of *Māyā* strewed the void not only with things knowable, but also with beings capable of knowledge in varying degrees; the summit of these degrees, for our world at least, is man, and his sufficient reason is to see things as only an intelligence capable of objectivity, synthesis and transcendence can see them.

We have said that the Substance "willed" and "had to" manifest the world; now in God "to will" and "to have to" coincide, if by these words one understands respectively Freedom and Necessity — the first perfection referring to Infinitude and the second to Absoluteness — for in God there is neither constraint nor arbitrariness. For most theologians, however, God seems perfect only if His willings are gratuitous; the subjective fact that man cannot grasp all the motives of the Divine Activity seems in their minds to amount to an objective divine characteristic, in other words, it practically signifies a divine right to arbitrariness

37

and tyranny. But obviously this is contrary to God's Perfection which implies fundamental Goodness as well as Beauty and Beatitude.

The Koranic saying "My Clemency precedeth my Wrath" allows of a very important and even fundamental cosmological application, from the point of view of the microcosm as well as of the macrocosm. "Wrath" or "Rigor" does not pertain to the absolute Substance; it pertains to the degree of the "Energies" and intervenes only in the formal world, either around us or within us; if man pierces this layer and proceeds into the superior layer — "the Kingdom of Heaven is within you" — he escapes the regimen of Rigor. One has to break the ice, which is possible only with God's help; once the soul has reached the underlying water, no further breaking-through is possible; the noise of outwardness is followed by the silence of inwardness. It "follows" but in reality it is before us; the soul enters into it as into a stream without origin or end; stream of silence, but also of music or light.

But let us return to the veil of *Māyā* strewing the void both with things and with beings capable of knowing them. Where there are objects, there are subjects: that is why in Being there is an objective and passive pole, the principial *Materia, Prakrti,* and a subjective or active pole, the manifesting, determining and diversifying *Spiritus,* namely *Purusha;* and the same holds true, *mutatis mutandis,* at each level of the Universe. However, if we start from the idea that the Substance is the Self, the infinite and absolute Subject[1] whose Object is on the one hand its own

1. The Absolute and the Infinite are complementary, the first being exclusive and the second inclusive: the Absolute excludes all that is contingent, and the Infinite includes all that is. Within contingency, the Absolute gives rise to perfection, and the Infinite to indefiniteness: the sphere is perfect, space is indefinite. Descartes reserved the term infi-

Infinitude and on the other its Universal Unfolding, there is no scission into subject and object on any ontological plane whatever; there will always be only one and the same Subject at multiple degrees of objectivation or exteriorization, for in this case the Subject is not a complementary pole, it is simply That which is. If we nonetheless term it "Subject," it is to express that *Ātmā* is the absolute Witness, at once transcendent and immanent, of all things, and that it is in no wise an unconscious, albeit energetic, Substance, as the pantheists and deists imagine. Furthermore, when the perception of the Object is so intense that the consciousness of the subject vanishes, the Object becomes Subject, as is the case in the union of love; but then the word "subject" no longer has the meaning of a complement that is fragmentary by definition; it means on the contrary a totality which we conceive as subjective because it is conscious.

When we place the emphasis on objective Reality — which then takes precedence in the relation between the subject and the object — the subject becomes object in the sense that, being determined entirely by the object, it forgets the element consciousness; in this case the subject, inasmuch as it is a fragment, is absorbed by the Object inasmuch as it is totality, just as the accident is reintegrated into the Substance. But the other manner of seeing things,

nite for God alone, whereas Pascal spoke of many infinites. One has to agree with Descartes, yet without blaming Pascal, for the absolute meaning of the word does not result from its literal meaning; the images are physical before being metaphysical, even though the causal relationship is inverse. Theology teaches that God is infinitely good and infinitely just since He is infinite, which is contradictory if one wished to be too particular, for an infinite quality in the absolute sense would exclude any other quality.

39

which reduces everything to the Subject, takes precedence over the point of view that grants primacy to the Object: if we adore God, it is not for the simple reason that He presents Himself to us as an objective reality of a dizzying and crushing immensity — otherwise we would adore the stars and nebulae — but it is above all because this reality, a priori objective, is the greatest of subjects; because He is the absolute Subject of our contingent subjectivity; because He is the at once all-powerful, omniscient and essentially benefic Consciousness. The subject as such takes precedence over the object as such: the consciousness of a creature capable of conceiving the starry heavens is more than the space and the stars so conceived; the argument that the senses can perceive a subject superior to our own is without value, for the senses always perceive merely the objective appearance, not subjectivity as such. In the world, the objective element, a priori virtual, came before the subjective element capable of actualizing it by perception — Genesis testifies to this; whereas in the principial order, the subjective comes before the objective; this the world retraces in an inverse sense, precisely, since it is as it were a reflective surface.

According to the Advaitic perspective, the element "object" is always internal in relation to an element "subject," so that things — including subjects insofar as they become objects owing to their contingency — are the imaginations, or the dreams of a subject that clearly transcends them: the formal world, for example, is the dream of a particularized Divine Consciousness that envelops and penetrates it. The Hindus have the tendency to affirm too easily — if only by way of ellipsis — that the world is merely in our mind, which suggests the solipsist error, namely that it is we who create the world by imagining it. But it is obviously not the creature — itself a content of the cosmic dream — who is the imagining subject; rather, the subject is He who dreams the world: it is *Buddhi,* projection of *Ātmā,* the "archangelic Consciousness," if one

40

will. The individual merely imagines his own thoughts; he is powerless before those of the Gods.[2]

Having created the material world, God projected into it subjects capable of perceiving it, and finally He delegated man, who alone is capable of perceiving it totally, that is, in connection with its Cause or Substance; as a result, man is the measure of things, as all traditional doctrines attest. Man is situated, spatially speaking, between the "infinitely big" and the "infinitely small" — in Pascal's terminology — so that it is his subjectivity and not a quality of the objective world that creates the line of demarcation. If we feel minute in stellar space, it is solely because what is big is more accessible to us than what is small and thus rapidly escapes our senses; and such is the case because it is the big and not the small that reflects the Infinitude and Transcendence of God in relation to man. But all this is still only a symbol, for in a much more real manner man is a point of junction between two infinitely more important dimensions, namely the outward and the inward: it is precisely in virtue of the dimension of inwardness, which opens onto the Absolute and therefore the Infinite, that man is quasi-divine.[3] Man is at once subject and object: he is a subject in relation to the world which he perceives and in relation to the Invisible which he conceives, but he is an object in relation to his "own Self"; the empirical ego is a content, hence an object, of the pure subject or of the ego-principle, and all the more so in relation to the immanent divine Subject which, in the final analysis, is our true "Self". This leads us to the Advaitic

2. We use this plural in order to specify that the direct Subject of the world is a projection — differentiated while remaining one — of the Self, and not the Self itself in a direct manner.

3. "The Kingdom of Heaven," which objectively is "above us" like the visible sky which reflects it, is, however, really or more concretely "within us," to paraphrase the Gospel. Elevation implies, requires and gives rise to depth.

question "Who am I?" made famous by Shri Ramana Maharshi; I am neither this body, nor this soul, nor this intelligence; what alone remains is *Ātmā*.

Man is thus called upon to choose — by definition as it were — between the outward and the inward; the outward is compressive dispersion and death, the inward, dilating concentration and life. Our relationship with space furnishes a symbol of this hostile nature of outwardness: by launching himself into planetary space — in fact or in principle — man becomes enclosed in a cold, despairing, mortal night, with neither up nor down and without end. Moreover, the same is true of all scientific investigation that goes beyond what is normal for man in light of the law of equilibrium that rules him ontologically.[4] By contrast, when man advances towards the inward, he enters into a welcoming and peace-giving limitlessness, fundamentally happy although not easy to achieve in fact; for it is only through deifying inwardness, whatever its price, that man is perfectly in conformity with his nature. The paradox of the human condition is that nothing is so contrary to us as the requirement to transcend ourselves, and nothing so fundamentally ourselves as the essence of this requirement, or the fruit of this transcending. The illogi-

---

4. The protagonists of so-called "exact" experimental science can be reproached, not with having discovered or grasped a given situation of the physical world, but with having enclosed themselves in a scientific curiosity that is disproportionate in relation to what is essentially knowable, hence with having forgotten man's total vocation. For this very reason, the pioneers of scientism never understood that humanity in general is intellectually and morally incapable of confronting data contrary to the collective and immemorial human experience; nor did they understand that the science of the relative, which by definition is partial, cannot detach itself with impunity from the science of the Absolute, which by definition is total. Galileo, and through him Copernicus, was accused of heresy, just as Aristarchus was accused well before them, and for the same reason, of "disturbing the tranquility of the Gods"; which is plausible when one takes into account all of the factors in question, for man is not made for astronomy alone.

cality of all egoism is to want to be oneself without wanting to be so altogether, hence without wanting to go beyond the empirical ego and its desires; or it is to relate everything to oneself, but without becoming interiorized, that is: without relating oneself to the Self.[5] All human absurdity lies in this contradiction.

*

*   *

Liberating inwardness, or the need for interiorization, follows from the very notion of Substance, or more precisely from our comprehension of this notion, which amounts to saying that the idea of Unity liberates when it is accepted with all of its consequences, that is, in accordance with sincerity of faith.[6] To grasp the nature of the one Substance — one, hence both unique and total — is first of all a thought: it is thus a complementary opposition between a subject and an object. But this duality is contrary to the very content of the thought of Unity: in objectifying the one Reality, we do not grasp it aright; it is an error comparable, not to a square that is supposed to represent a circle, but to a circle that is supposed to be identical with a sphere. It is a dimensional, not an essential, error; in a domain wherein the sphere alone is efficacious, the circle is all but inoperative, although it is the shadow of the sphere and although within two-dimension-

---

5. As regards "egoism" let us specify that we contrast it, not with an "altruism" that is sentimental and lacking in sufficient reason, but with the self-love that results simply from the right to exist and the duty to realize the meaning of existence. "Love thy neighbor as thyself" means that one must love oneself, but in accordance with God.

6. The inestimable value of the idea of the Absolute enables one to understand the Islamic axiom — at first sight exorbitant — of salvation through the notion of the Divine Unity; every sin can be pardoned, except the rejection of Unity, this Unity being none other than the Substance.

ality it is identified with the sphere as truth is identified with reality.

At the level of thought, the Substance can indeed be conceived, but it cannot be reached. Consequently, thought is an imperfect and provisional adequation, at least in a certain respect; at this level, the apprehension of Unity stops midway, so to speak. The truth of the One Substance can be realized only in the Heart, where the opposition between a knowing subject and an object to be known is transcended, or in other words, where all objectification — limitative by definition — is reduced to its unlimited source within infinite Subjectivity itself. The objective manifestations of the transcendent Substance are discontinuous in relation to It; it is only in the Heart that there is continuity between consciousness and the immanent Substance, whether virtually, or effectively.

In other words, and at the risk of repeating ourselves: although the Divine Substance is beyond the polarity of subject and object — or, although the Divine Substance, being the absolute Subject, is itself its own Object — we necessarily conceive it as an objective reality, even though it is transcendent or abstract. Now this conception, however metaphysically consistent, is imperfect and in a sense inadequate, precisely because it implies the separation between a subject and an object, and thus is not really proportioned to its content, which is absolutely simple and unpolarized. The passage from distinctive or mental consciousness to unitive or cardiac consciousness is a consequence of the very content of thought: either we understand imperfectly what the notions of the Absolute, Infinite, Essence, Substance, Unity mean, so that we are satisfied with concepts, and this is what is done by philosophers in the conventional sense of the word; or else we understand these notions perfectly, so that they oblige us by their very content to transcend conceptual separativeness by seeking the Real in the depths of the Heart, not as an adventure, but with the aid of traditional means without which we can

44

do nothing and have no right to anything; for "Whoso gathereth with Me not, scattereth." The transcendent and exclusive Substance then reveals itself as immanent and inclusive.

It could also be said that God being All that is, we must know Him with all that we are: and to know Him who is infinitely lovable — since nothing is lovable except through Him — is to love Him infinitely.[7]

---

7. "Lo, verily, not for the love of the husband is a husband dear, but for love of the Self in him. Lo, verily, not for the love of the wife is a wife dear, but for love of the Self in her." *(Brihadaranyaka Upanishad,* IV, 5,6). "It is *Ātmā* alone who must be loved. For him that loveth *Ātmā* alone, that which he holdeth dear is not perishable." *(ibid.* I, 4, 8). "Thou shalt love the Lord thy God with all thy heart, and with all thy soul, and with all thy mind." *(Matthew,* XXII, 37).

Creation as a Divine Quality

According to the Hindus and the Greeks the world amounts to a Divine Quality, in the sense that it is an ontologically necessary manifestation of God and therefore participates in the divine Eternity; and this is so even though manifestation essentially comprises a rhythm, consisting in a chain of ever new and different "creations." Like the Creator, this chain has neither beginning nor end, which means that the Universe is conceived as a permanent cycle of impermanent "creations," or as a "coeternal" cycle of temporal worlds.

According to the monotheist Semites, the Christians included, the world does not have this aspect of coeternity; it proceeds, not from a necessity of the divine Nature, but from a free act of God; it is something that need not be, and it has a beginning but no end, because God has so decided. The explanation of this enigma is that the Semites, who are "humanists" and moralists before being metaphysicians, take into consideration only one cycle, hence they are right in accepting only one creation; total cosmic manifestation, coeternal, therefore, with God, could not be of interest to them — except on the plane of esoterism — given precisely that their perspective is a kind of "nationalism of the human condition."[1]

---

1. The average Semitic spirit is interested less in what "is" objectively, than in what "is indispensable" subjectively; quite aside from questions of ethnic complexity and of esoterism.

As we have just indicated, cosmic and coeternal manifestation is necessary because God is necessary, whereas "creation" is free because it is not "the manifestation" but "a manifestation." God is in fact free in His "modes of expression," but not in His "ways of being," so to speak, and this is necessarily the case since the perfection of freedom and the perfection of necessity must both be found in the divine Nature; despite the anthropomorphist theologians who see a constraint in necessity, and who unconsciously confuse freedom with arbitrariness, hence with the absence of principles.

Indeed, God was not obliged to create "this" world, that is to say, these minerals, these plants, these animals; but by His very Nature He was obliged to create "the world as such": by His very Nature, that is, by virtue of the Radiation demanded by His being the "Good."

Perhaps we ought to repeat here — because of its doctrinal importance — the thesis we have formulated above: starting from the idea that the Supreme Principle is at once absolute and infinite, we shall specify that being absolute, It is the only Reality, and that, being infinite, It is All-Possibility. Now in Its manifestation, the Absolute is affirmed by existence and by the substances that concretize It; the Infinite is manifested correlatively by space and time, and by the limitless diversity of their contents. The Good as such is manifested in all this by positive phenomena — whether by creatures, things, faculties or qualities — and it is manifested indirectly and *a contrario* — hence in privative and contrasting mode — by negative phenomena, which indicate remoteness from the Divine Source; a remoteness that is caused, precisely, by manifesting or creative Radiation, hence by the cosmogonic process.

Or again: the number one, the geometric point, the circle and the sphere manifest the Absolute, that is, the Good in its aspect of Absoluteness; correlatively, the indefinite series of numbers and complex geometric shapes and

48

forms manifest the Infinite, that is, the Good in its aspect of Infinitude. However, within this series, the trace of the Absolute is always freshly reaffirmed by the numbers, planimetric shapes and three-dimensional forms that recapitulate respectively unity, the point, the circle and the sphere. To give just one example: in the numerical order there is the number three which, within the expansion of Possibility, marks an initial return to Unity.

The Augustinian idea that the good tends by its very nature to communicate itself, is at bottom Platonic: this idea is self-evident since, according to Plato, the Absolute is by definition the "Sovereign Good," the *Agathón*, and to say "Good," is to say Radiation or Manifestation. And that is why in Islam the second Name of God is the "infinitely Merciful," *Raḥmān;* it is in virtue of His *Raḥmah* that God created the world, He who "was a hidden treasure" and who "wished to be known," according to a *hadīth*. In the *Vedānta*, the idea of the "Sovereign Good" springs from the ternary *Sat, Chit, Ānanda:* "Being," "Consciousness," "Beatitude"; the third term coinciding with All-Possibility, hence with Radiation. If there were no *Māyā*, *Ātmā* would not be *Ātmā*.

*

*　*

A crucial point in Semitic creationism is the idea that God created the world "out of nothing," *ex nihilo*. On this subject, we have the following observations to make: only an altogether artificial logic would treat the word *ex*, in the expression *creatio ex nihilo*, as if it indicated that nothingness is implicitly considered as a "thing," hence as something which absurdly "preexists" creation. In reality the word *ex* pertains exclusively to the structure of the language, it therefore cannot prove an idea. Since language is made to take into account what exists, one cannot ask grammatical means to be appropriate to what does not exist. The word *nihil* expresses the absence of existence or reality, and that is all; it is perfectly clear, and excludes in advance the risk that nothingness could take on the function of a "thing" or an "object." God created the world out of nothing, that is, He did not draw it out of any preexisting element; now nothingness could not be "preexistent" in any sense, since precisely it means inexistence.[2]

We must insist: the fact that "inexistence" is a word, hence something existent, in no way implies that what is inexistent could be conceived as existent by anyone who can think; to say that "God made the world out of nothing" does not mean, despite the word *ex*, that from "nothingness" He took "something," as men take some material when they fashion some utensil or work of art. It is because one understands quite naturally what the word "nothing" means that it is used, and that the Holy Spirit was the first to use it; if the Spirit had not wished the word *nihil* to be understood literally, it would have employed another word.[3]

A priori therefore, the word *nihil* means "nothing"; but a posteriori and according to an esoteric interpretation, the same word can mean that which, while being real, nonetheless does not exist at the level of the world, and thus this "real" could only refer to God.[4] For if the world is

---

2. If one were to say *emanatio ex Deo*, the word *ex* would indicate an ontological causality; but in *creatio ex nihilo*, it merely indicates a logical relationship. It should be noted that in *creatio ex nihilo*, the words *ex nihilo* merely serve to specify the notion of *creatio*, *creatio* being *ex nihilo* by definition.

3. ". . . Look at the heaven and the earth and see all that is in them, and know that God hath made them out of nothing . . ." (*II Maccabees*, VII, 28). In the same way, all the Credos — they too inspired by the Holy Spirit — teach *creatio ex nihilo*.

4. ". . . All possibilities are included in total Possibility, which is one with the Principle itself . . . Therefore, if manifestation proceeds from these possibilities, . . . it does not come from something exterior to the Principle . . . ." (René Guénon, "Création et Manifestation," in *Etudes Traditionnelles*, Oct. 1937).

defined as "something," God, who is not this "something," will seem to be "nothing." We may express this distinction between the two meanings of the word *nihil* — one literal and necessary and the other transposed and possible — also in the following way: according to the proper meaning of the word, *nihil* means that which, being nothing, is so to speak "below" existence; according to an esoteric interpretation — which, moreover, violates the proper meaning of the word — *nihil* is on the contrary that which, being principial and hence non-manifested, is "above" existence, that is, above Manifestation, and consequently that which absurdly appears to be "nothing" from the level of Manifestation.

*

* *

Positively speaking, the world is created by the Word; the *creatio ex nihilo* then gives way to *creatio per Verbum:* "All things were made by him; and without him was not anything made that was made," teaches the Gospel of John.[5] *Creatio ex nihilo per Verbum* evokes, by its two parts — one negative and the other positive — this mysterious formula of the Song of Songs: "I am black, but beautiful"; and also the Testimony of Faith of Islam, which also comprises two parts at once antinomic and complementary: "There is no divinity, if not the (only) Divinity."

The creative Word can be understood at two levels, and it is this "fluctuation" which explains the all but general incomprehension, on the part of theologians, of the Platonic "demiurge." In the first place, the Word is situated at the degree of the ontological Principle, Being, of which it is

5. This is what Genesis expresses through the often repeated formula "God said."

the active pole, the Vedantic *Purusha;*[6] it is the divine Intellect which conceives the possibilities of manifestation or the archetypes. Next, at the very center of universal Manifestation, there is the operative reflection of *Purusha,* namely *Buddhi,* the manifested and acting Word; and this is the demiurge proper. This *Buddhi* is the "Spirit of God which moved upon the waters," while the divine *Purusha* remains immutable, since it pertains to pure Being; but, as we have said, Being is mirrored at the center of Existence — as *Buddhi,* precisely — in order to become efficient. And let us recall here these phrases of David: "By the word of the Lord were the heavens made; and all the host of them by the breath of his mouth . . . For he spake, and it was done; he commanded, and it stood fast." *(Psalms* XXXIII, 6 and 9).[7]

That is to say: just as principial *Māyā* is bipolarized into *Purusha* and *Prakrti,* so manifested *Māyā* comprises two poles, namely the active and imaginative demiurge and the passive but efficient Substance; it is this *materia prima* which is the *tohu wa bohu* of Genesis or the *khaos* — the "void" — of Hesiod's theogony. Let it be noted that the Greek word *khaos* has the double meaning of "primordial abyss" and "indeterminate matter"; it is neither nothingness pure and simple nor a substance preceding the creative act, but, together with the demiurge, the first content of creation; the active demiurge being the center, and its passive complement, the periphery. This two-fold

6. The inseparable passive pole being *Prakrti,* the principial Substance or the "Divine Femininity"; the "Mother of all beings."

7. It has also been translated: "He spoke, and it was born; he ordained, and it was there." The first result doubtless signifies conception in the divine Intellect — hence the possibilities conceived by *Purusha,* Being — and the second result, the creative effectuation by *Buddhi.*

demiurge constitutes the creative power in the midst of creation itself.

It is the passive aspect of the demiurge that we recognize in the "Water" of the Akkadian-Babylonians, notwithstanding their parallel concept of a creative "Father" *(Apsu)* and a creative "Mother" *(Tiamat)*. The "Water" of Thales is also identified with the first Substance; the same is true of the "Infinite" *(Apeiron)* of Anaximander, as well as of the "Fire" of Heraclitus. It is probable however that these diverse concepts apply to the level of divinity as well as to the cosmic level, and thus to the Divine Being as well as to the demiurge. All this, of course, has nothing to do with the logical and totally negative *nihil* of the *creatio ex nihilo;* but if one absolutely insists on giving a positive sense to the word *nihil* — contrary to its proper sense, and by symbolical transposition — there are two possible interpretations, namely the "Divine Nothingness" and the "celestial nothingness," God and the demiurge; in no case could it refer to Beyond-Being — the pure Absolute — which is not involved in creation.

The profound explanation of the myths of the "sinful" woman, "prisoner" of chthonic powers, "ravished" by a demon, "swallowed" by the earth, or even become infernal — Eve, Eurydice, Sita, Izanami, according to case — this explanation doubtless is to be found in the scission between the male demiurge and the female demiurge, or between the center and the periphery of the cosmos; this periphery being envisaged then, not as the cosmic substance as such, which remains virgin in relation to its productions, but as the totality of these productions; for it is the accidents, and not the substance, which comprise "evil" in all its forms. But, aside from the fact that the substance remains virgin even while being mother, it is redeemed at the very level of its exteriorization through its positive contents, which are in principle sacramental and saving; symbolically speaking, if "woman" was lost through choosing "matter" or the "world," she was redeemed — and is redeemed — through giving birth to the *Avatāra*.[8] And besides, "every thing is *Ātmā*"; and "it is not for the love of the husband (or of the wife or the son) that the husband (or the wife or the son) is dear, but for the love of *Ātmā* which is in him." That is, the feminine element — the Substance — is by definition a mirror of the Essence,[9] despite its exteriorizing and alienating function; moreover, a mirror is necessarily separated from what it reflects, and therein lies its ambiguity.

*

* *

The most direct and hence complete expression of the cosmogonic mystery is unquestionably the Hindu doctrine; therefore it is to this doctrine, and not to the Semitic esoterisms, that one should have recourse in the first place in order to have a full explanation. The essence of this doctrine is the idea of *Māyā*. It is the idea of universal Relativity; and it is precisely this idea which not only the Semites but also the western Aryans lack, with the exception of esoterists, including a priori Platonists;[10] nevertheless

8. When Saint Paul says that woman gains salvation through the function of childbearing, he implicitly evokes this mystery. The point of view is different when he advocates the ideal of virginity: in this case, woman participates, not in the positive creative function, but in the inviolable purity of the Substance.

9. In fact, the terms "substance" and "essence" are often synonymous, but strictly speaking, the first term suggests a continuity, and the second, a discontinuity; the first refers more to immanence, and the second, to transcendence. On the one hand, one distinguishes between the substance, which is permanent, and the "accidents," which change; on the other hand, one makes a distinction between the essence, which is the fundamental nature — whether it is a question of the Principle or of manifestation — and the "form," which is its reflection or mode of expression.

10. The notion of *Māyā* is essentially contained in the Platonic distinction between contingent things and the "ideas," the pure archetypes.

Western antiquity, classical or other, possessed a cosmology close to that of the Hindus.

Now *Māyā* encompasses by definition all that directly or indirectly concerns the mystery of "creation": consequently it encompasses both *Purusha* and *Buddhi*, that is to say, the "Word" at the metacosmic as well as at the cosmic level; in short, it encompasses the Creator as well as the creature, "God" as well as the "world"; only the "pure Absolute," "Beyond-Being," *Parabrahma* or *Ātmā*, escapes its grasp. It is this "pure Absolute" that by its nature determines *Māyā;* but *Māyā* cannot determine *Ātmā* in any way, whereas *Māyā* determines God, the creative Person; without whom there could be no creation.

The doctrine of Relativity or of "Illusion," or of the "Divine Magic," is joined to that of cosmic cycles: the world, or the manifested universe, the creation, therefore, is like the "breathing" of the Divinity; it is essentially subject to phases, to "divine lives," as the Hindus would say. There is firstly the *para,* which is the "life" of the demiurge itself and which lasts one hundred "years of *Brahmā*"; the "days of *Brahmā*" — the *kalpas* — each represent the duration of a world, hence a "historical creation," the "night of *Brahmā*" being the "divine void" between two creations *ex nihilo.* Each *kapla* comprises one thousand *mahā-yugas,* each of which is divided into four ages or *yugas,* namely: the *krita-,* the *treta-,* the *dvāpara-* and the *kali-yuga;* these are, analogically speaking, the golden age, the silver age, the bronze age and the iron age. Doubtless, there are variations in the different cosmological symbolisms of India, but the fundamental pattern remains identical. Be that as it may, what matters essentially is to know that the world is an "optical illusion," and that this illusion necessarily comprises modes and cycles, as is shown, moreover, by the modes and cycles of nature around and within us. The universal modes and cycles are so to speak the marks of Relativity, by their very diversity and plurality; to the Principle alone belongs the glory of being simple and unique. We could also say that "creation as such" — the invariability of the existential phenomenon and the coeternal chain of the cycles — attests to the Divine Necessity, while a particular creation — a given mode and cycle — attests to the Divine Freedom; although from another point of view, and quite evidently, Necessity and Freedom are everywhere combined.

*

* *

The *Vedānta* distinguishes between a "pure" *Māyā* that projects the expanse of space-time and that is none other than the personal God *(Ishvara),* and an "impure" *Māyā,* that brings about the diversification of phenomena as well as existential ignorance *(avidya),* and that most directly appears in the form of the individual soul *(jīvātmā),* subjectively speaking at least; but all this pertains to cosmology — and in part to anthropology — more than cosmogony, which alone interests us here.[11] We shall nonetheless indicate that manifested *Māyā* — microcosmic as well as macrocosmic — is conceived as divided into different "states" or "envelopes," according to their degree of relativity or exteriorization, and these are, analogically and symbolically: the "waking" state *(vaishvānara),* the "dream" state *(taijasa),* the state of "deep sleep" *(prājna),* and then the "fourth" state *(turīya)* which corresponds to the absolutely unlimited Consciousness of the Supreme Self *(Paramātmā).* It is the very importance of the idea of *Māyā* that obliges us to mention here these diverse modes which, being fundamental, necessarily concern cosmogony as well: on the one hand, each world and each creature is situated at one of these degrees — while possibly

11. It should be noted that Hindu concepts are often more indicative than systematically consistent, in the sense that the authors intend to furnish keys rather than strictly concordant notions; in fact, this remark applies to most Oriental doctrines.

realizing several of them as regards its constitution — and on the other hand, the cosmogonic projection is brought about from the inmost degree towards the exterior;[12] it could be said: towards nothingness, if nothingness had a reality other than a purely indicative one.

Instead of distinguishing only between a Relativity that is "pure" and another that is "impure" — the one being principial and the other phenomenal — we could also distinguish, and this is even essential, between a Relativity that is "ascending" and another that is "descending," and then admit a third, situated between these two, and which is "horizontal." This scheme corresponds to the ternary of the universal qualities *(gunas)*: "luminosity" or "lightness" *(sattva)*, "obscurity" or "heaviness" *(tamas)*, and between them, "heat" or "expansivity" *(rajas)*. Thus there is a *Māyā* which is divine and attracts to God, another which is satanic and takes away from God, and an intermediary one which a priori is innocently passional and seeks only to be itself, so that it remains provisionally neutral in relation to the other two qualities. The manifestations of these three tendencies are either static or dynamic, relating respectively to "forms" or to "movements," and all this at diverse levels.

Let us also note — and this follows from traditional concepts — that the degrees or modes of *Māyā* can be envisaged either as subjectivities or as objective principles or phenomena, according to whether they are conceived in terms of the pole "Consciousness" or the pole "Being." Thus, for example, there is a relation of analogy between the waking state *(vaishvānara)* and the body, or between the dream state *(taijasa)* and the soul, all of which is prefi-

---

12. This is what evolutionism ignores out of principle, since for it each species proceeds, not from the interior towards the exterior and each independently of the other, but rather on the exterior, starting from the preceding species; inwardness is denied deliberately, and with it the world of "ideas" or archetypes.

gured in the universal order; the microcosm and the macrocosm are a unity, so much so that all matter is our body, and all the psychic substance is our soul.

*

* *

One may be tempted to conclude, from the fact that the Creator as well as the creature are included in *Māyā*, that the discontinuity between them is merely relative; but it is rather a "relatively absolute" discontinuity that should be spoken of in this case. The absolute discontinuity between existence and Beyond-Being — or the Essence — is reflected on the plane of universal Relativity, and this reflection will be the "relatively absolute" discontinuity between existence and Being, the creature and the Creator, the world and God. If it be objected that a "relatively absolute" distance does not step out of Relativity, and therefore that the gap still remains relative, we reply that in this case, more than in any other analogous and ontologically subordinate case, the very reason for this distance is its character of absoluteness, which it is necessary to specify on pain of suggesting serious errors and of sacrificing the dimension of transcendence to that of immanence.

In other words: if the discontinuity between creation and the Creator is relative on account of *Māyā* which encompasses both the Cause and the effect, it is nonetheless absolute on account of the transcendence of the Principle in relation to Manifestation.

*

* *

To creative exteriorization, which proceeds from the center to the periphery, responds an initiatory or mystical interiorization, which proceeds in the inverse direction, and whose psychological prefiguration is virtue. Actually, virtue tends from the accidental towards the substantial or from the contingent form to the archetype, to the "idea," whose essence is the Sovereign Good, the *Agathón*. The same holds true for art, whose purpose is to transfer the archetype into contingency; and this is true "realism," since the real lies above us, and not below us as the moderns would have it. But it goes without saying that artistic expression is no more than the prefiguration of spiritual alchemy, whose matter is the soul and which realizes, inwardly and in a fundamental manner, what art demonstrates and promises at the level of immediate perceptions and emotions.[13] The artist brings the Divine into the world; the mystic reintegrates the world — his soul — into the Divine; always with the help of Heaven, for "Without me ye can do nothing."

13. This relationship between art and spirituality allows of understanding how art or artisanry can be the vehicle of contemplation; it accounts for the artisanal initiations, without forgetting, on a different but nonetheless analogous plane, the initiations based upon the martial arts.

The Onto-Cosmological Chain

We have spoken more than once about ontological projection and the bipolarization it implies, but we may not have explained sufficiently this bipolarization inasmuch as it is manifested at each level of the cosmos, in virtue of the existentiating projection precisely. The trajectory as a whole can be represented, geometrically speaking, as a "descending" chain of triangles which are alternately upright and upside-down,[1] the former indicating an intrinsic polarity, and the latter a "production" and a change of degree, thus an extrinsic dimension.

The first triangle-symbol represents the Sovereign Good inasmuch as it comprises the two aspects of Absoluteness and Infinitude;[2] this first bipolarity projects — so to speak — creative and personal Being thus "engendering" the second triangle, which is upside-down because the duality is situated at the summit and the unity at the base.

Being itself gives rise in its turn to a new bipolarization, namely creative Inspiration and receptive Substance

1. Both positions are combined in the Seal of Solomon.
2. This first polarity, by the nature of things, possesses widely distant and diverse reflections and applications: thus, a definition must express, on the one hand "only the thing defined" and on the other hand "the whole of the thing defined"; hence unicity and totality, absoluteness and infinitude. The applications are multiple and diverse in virtue of the universality of the principles which they project or manifest.

61

which is both virginal and maternal; this is the couple *Purusha* and *Prakrti,* the Masculine and the Feminine at the level of Being, and this couple, together with Being itself, constitutes the third triangle in the cosmogonic chain.

This principial couple engenders the manifested Logos and together with it constitutes the fourth triangle; next comes, at the level of the Logos, the fifth triangle, owing to the fact that the Logos for its part also comprises two aspects, one active or masculine and the other passive or feminine: these two aspects are, on the one hand, the Universal Intellect at the center of the cosmos, and on the other hand, the Universal Substance, both virgin and mother; it is from them that arise all the phenomena that make up the world.

The bipolarization of the Logos, together with the world that it projects, or that it produces, so to speak, constitute a sixth triangle, which is upside-down because there is a production; and the world in its turn comprises a new triangle owing to the fact that it too implies a bipolarity, namely an "essence" and a "substance" which on the physical plane become "energy" and "matter"; pure matter being nothing other than the ether. Thus we have arrived at the final outcome, or at the "lowest" point, of the onto-cosmological projection; at least from the point of view of the world in which we find ourselves, for one can conceive of limit-worlds still more remote from the starting point than ours, or on the contrary less remote. "And God knoweth best," as the Moslems would say; to know principles is one thing, to know modalities is another.

Absoluteness and Infinitude: we could also say: Necessity and Possibility;[3] their one essence being the Supreme Good, and their common function, the Projection of this Good in the direction of Relativity.

---

3. Or Necessity and Freedom, according to a somewhat different point of view. To return to the domain of applications: when man loves

*

* *

The fact that the cosmogonic trajectory — the rhythm of Relativity, in other words — is brought about in relation with the trinity and not some other Pythagorean number is not fortuitous in any way: the number three, by its very asymmetry, is in fact the number of progression or movement; neither the Christian Trinity nor other analogous Trinities would have any meaning without a "creation" that proceeds from them and that they prefigure intrinsically. It is true that there is not only the geometric trinity, the triangle, but that there is also trinity as such, which proceeds in a straight line and has nothing specifically creative about it, no more so at least than any other number; this trinity then signifies a hierarchy of values or a choice between two opposite elements. In the latter case, trinity comprises a center-measure, namely a qualitative distinction either between an "above" and a "below," or between a "rightwards" and a "leftwards"; the first of these distinctions being more radical than the second which implies a "common level" rather than a difference in levels.

But obviously it is not only the number three — or the triangle — which governs the structure of the Universe; the Supreme Principle — mathematically speaking — also has an aspect of duality and an aspect of quaternity, and even more complex aspects; and the same holds true for the Universe, both as such and at each of its levels. The meaning of duality is that of complementary harmony or, more relatively, that of opposition, or both things at once; as for quaternity, it refers to a finished "universe,"

---

woman, it is as if necessity tended towards possibility or liberty; in feminine love, it is on the contrary possibility or freedom which seeks the support of necessity.

whether *in divinis* or at the level of the world. Whereas duality "engenders" and trinity "projects" or "sets into motion," quaternity suffices unto itself, it is a result or an achievement; it is the number of stability, a quality that has the square is its fundamental geometric symbol.

Just as trinity comprises a static as well as a dynamic aspect, so too does quaternity — while geometrically indicating the principle of stability — contain within itself an aspect of movement, and this is the unfolding of cyclic phases, whether in an ascending or descending direction; if on the one hand there is, in relation to the Principle-Origin, a withdrawal and a separation, on the other hand there is a return and a reintegration. Both directions moreover can coincide: from the purely earthly point of view, youth is an expansion, and old age a decline; whereas from the spiritual point of view youth is, in general, the time of passions and illusions, and old age that of wisdom and thus of a new springtime.

Dimensions of Omnipotence

According to a famous argument, one of two things is true: either God wishes to destroy evil but cannot, in which case He is not omnipotent; or else He can abolish evil but does not wish to do so, in which case He is not good. Our readers know our answer: God can abolish a given evil, but not evil as such; any evil, but not the very possibility of evil. For the possibility of evil is contained within All-Possibility, over which God — the creative Personal God — has no power, since All-Possibility belongs to the Divine Essence itself, and the Essence comes "before" the Person; Beyond-Being or Non-Being comes "before" Being; the Suprapersonal Divinity determines the Personal God, and not the other way round.

We have quoted elsewhere the Augustinian postulate that it is in the nature of the good to communicate itself. Beyond-Being, the essence of all good — and thus the Sovereign Good itself — possesses the intrinsic quality of radiation; but to radiate is, on the one hand, to communicate a good and, on the other, to move away from its source; every good that the world offers us comes from radiation and every evil, from remoteness. But the good of radiation compensates for the evil of remoteness, and this is proved by the Apocatastasis which brings every evil back to the initial Good. In the total Universe and in the procession of the cosmic cycles, evil is reduced to an almost fleeting accident, no matter how important it may be to those beings who undergo it or witness it.

This may also be expressed as follows, and as we have done on more than one occasion: the Absolute by definition comprises the "energy" or *"shakti"* that is Infinitude, and, as All-Possibility, it projects Relativity, *Māyā*. Now, the Personal God is the center or the very summit of this extrinsic dimension; far from being able to determine the Absolute-Infinite, His function is to bring about and govern existential projection; it is with regard to this projection that God as Creator, Legislator and Retributor is omnipotent and appears to be the Absolute itself. And God is "good" by virtue of His Essence whose potentialities, including those that are properly His, He manifests. Every good that we meet with in the world bears witness both to the Divine Essence and to its "personification", whereas evil only bears witness to it by opposition and privation.

To summarize again: the Supreme Principle, being absolute, and thereby infinite, is essentially what — by analogy with every conceivable good — we may call the "Sovereign Good." This Good, as we have said, has to communicate itself by reason of the inner logic of its nature; it must radiate and, as a consequence, must project a reflection which moves away from its source and proceeds in the direction of "nothingness." In reality, "nothingness" does not exist, except as a possibility of direction or tendency; as a "possibility of the impossible," one might say. The Supreme Principle contains All-Possibility, and thus cannot exclude the possibility of its own impossibility, to put it very paradoxically; but since this purely abstract possibility can never exist in or of itself, it is manifested — and is nothing more than this manifestation — in the mode of a tendency towards an obscure pole which is non-existent in itself. To be sure, this formulation is not intended to be exhaustive — no formulation could be — but it does nonetheless provide an adequate reference point; in metaphysics, that is all one can ask of human thought.[1]

*

* *

The use of the term *"Māyā"* in the above passage — in reference to Relativity — gives us the opportunity to make the following points. There is no question of identifying *Māyā* with evil, although the opposition between good and evil is not entirely unrelated to the reciprocity *Ātmā-Māyā;* without *Māyā* there would be neither privation nor perversion, since evil is nothing but the extreme and obscure reflection of *Māyā,* the *shakti* of *Ātmā.*[2] In any event — and this is crucial — an essential distinction must be made between the *Māyā* that is divine *(= Ishvara),*[3] another that is celestial *(= Buddhi and Svarga),* and a third that humanly speaking is "earthly" but which, in reality, encompasses the whole domain of transmigration *(Samsāra),* the round of births and deaths. One can likewise distinguish in *Māyā* an objective mode, which refers to the universe surrounding us and partly transcending us, and a subjective mode which refers to the experiences of our ego;[4] in principle, man can act upon the magic of the world by dominating the magic of his soul.

1. This is what anti-metaphysical philosophers are fundamentally ignorant of, and that is why the ancient doctrines appear to them to be "dogmatic" or "naive" whereas they are all that doctrines can be: namely, "signs" that are conducive to actualizing immanent and latent intellections. It is at the very least paradoxical that those "thinkers" who are most unaware of their limitations and most duped by the products of their minds, should not even know what thought is or what purpose it serves.
2. This is what is expressed by the myth of the fall and the paradoxical name Lucifer (light-bearer) given to the genius of evil.
3. The supreme prefiguration of this already relative divine element being the potentially "overflowing" Infinitude of the Absolute.
4. This is Shakespeare's "stuff as dreams are made on," and coincides with that of the world.

67

Some near synonyms of the term *Māyā* — which roughly signifies "magic power" — are *līlā*, "play," and *moha*, "illusion"; *Mahā-Moha* is the "Great Illusion," namely Manifestation in its full extension, metacosmic as well as cosmic.

An observation is called for here: despite what the over-confident pseudo-Vedantist simplifiers may think, it is not possible to go beyond Relativity — in any relevant context — without the acquiescence and help of the Divine Relative, both of which are far from being given gratuitously, but on the contrary involve and demand all that we are.

*

* *

Much could be said about the operations and modalities of Divine Omnipotence. In the case of miracles, God projects something of Himself into the world and modifies the natural course of things by His Presence. In other cases, which properly speaking do not fall outside the natural course of things, the Divine Presence is less direct or, if one prefers, more indirect, for the entry of God into the world cannot mean that the Divine Presence enters the world with its very substance, which would reduce the world to ashes. This amounts to saying that in the sphere of the manifestations of Divine Power, one has to distinguish between "horizontal" and "vertical" dimensions, the vertical being supernatural and the horizontal natural; for the materialists, only the horizontal dimension exists, and that is why they cannot conceive of causes which operate vertically and which for that very reason are non-existent for them, like the vertical dimension itself.[5]

---

5. It may be pointed out here that the evolutionist error has its roots in this prejudice. Instead of conceiving that creatures are archetypes "incarnated" in matter, starting from the Divine Intellect and passing

Instead of the ideas of horizontality and verticality, one could also use the images of the circle and the cross, or of concentric circles and radii: on the one hand, causality is confined to the circles, and this is the natural order of things, devoid of mystery; on the other hand, causality emanates from the central point, and this is the supernatural order, miraculous and divine. "For men that is impossible; but for God, all things are possible."

*

* *

If God were good, argue the atheists and even certain deists, He would abolish evil. There are two answers to that, and the first has been given already: God cannot abolish evil as such because it results from All-Possibility, which is ontologically "prior" to the personal God; consequently, God can only abolish a particular evil to the extent that, in so doing, He takes account of the metaphysical necessity of evil in itself.[6] The second answer in a way goes beyond the first, to the point of appearing to contradict it: God, being good, in fact abolishes not only particular evils but also evil as such; particular evils because everything has an ending, and evil as such because, being subject in the last analysis to the same rule, it disappears as a result of the cosmic cycles and the effect of the Apocatastasis.[7] Thus the formula *vincit omnia Veritas* applies not only to Truth but also to the Good in all its aspects. And this means likewise that there can never be any symmetry

through a subtle or animic plane, they restrict all causality to the material world, deliberately ignoring the flagrant contradictions implied by this conceptual "planimetry."

6. What is ontologically necessary is, in Semitic parlance, "What is written."

7. In Hindu doctrine, the "night of *Brahmā*" follows the "day of *Brahmā*": after projection comes reintegration.

between Good and evil;[8] evil has no being in itself, whereas the Good is the being of all things. The Good is That which is; Being and the Good coincide.

Our second answer could incur the objection that its bearing is only relative since the cyclic limits do not abolish the possibility of evil which, in fact, has to reappear in some degree or another in the course of each cycle. That is true — while not being really an objection — and it leads us once more to the problem of the very nature of the Infinite, which implies that All-Possibility must by definition include the possibility of its own negation, to the extent, precisely, that this negation is possible; and it is possible, not, of course, at the actual level of the principle, but in an already very relative modality of contingency, thus at the lower extremity of *Māyā* and consequently in an "illusory" manner; that is to say unreal at the level of the Absolute.

The Divine Quality of Goodness[9] can be envisaged in different connections and at various levels: first of all, there is the Absolute as the "Sovereign Good" and, in consequence, as the supreme — but indirect — source of every possible good; next there is the "Sovereign Good" inasmuch as it is "personified" at the level of Being and within Being; more relatively there is the Divine Radiation, the cosmogonic function of the Good, the creative

---

8. It is by virtue of this principle that beauty, for example, is ontologically more real than ugliness — which is denied with typical passion by the modern mind, a mind that relativizes, subjectivizes and inverts everything — and it is again for this reason that the "golden age" lasts far longer than the other ages, especially the "iron age."

9. What we mean here by "Quality" is not simply an attribute depending on relativity, but an intrinsic characteristic of the Absolute; thus a reality inseparable from the Essence. It is to absolute "Goodness" that the Sanskrit term *Ānanda* refers, as do the Arabic words *Raḥmah* and *Raḥmān* which contain the nuances of "Beatitude," "Goodness," "Beauty" as well as of boundless Potentiality. "God is Love" say the Scriptures, which refers to these various aspects.

70

projection of the world; and lastly there is the final reintegration, the Apocatastasis. And we could likewise mention all the aspects of good which the Universe contains and which, either as a whole or separately, also constitute a manifestation of the Good as such; in this sense, every good is indirectly a theophany.

Some could reproach us for giving the notion of "evil" a metaphysical connotation, whereas in their eyes it has only a moral or sentimental one; with which we disagree, because we think we are right in calling "evil" something that opposes — or believes it is opposing — the Real. We are right in calling it evil insofar as it opposes the Real and consequently opposes our ultimate interests, but not necessarily in other respects; not in respect of its existence, in any case, nor again in respect of some function that is necessary for the equilibrium of the world.

The antagonism between Good and evil is in a way the combat between Being and nothingness, which is waged to the extent that Being lends to nothingness a certain existence, although always in the context of the necessary radiation of the Divine Self, which is, as stated by the Sufis, a "Message from Himself to Himself."

*

* *

According to Saint Paul, the Divine Wrath — or the Divine quality of Justice — must be able to manifest itself, and, consequently, there must be something that provokes it, which is expressed moreover by the saying: "Scandal must needs come . . ." From a somewhat different viewpoint one may say that the specific — and contrasting — good that is the victory over evil, or the deliverance from an evil, obviously presupposes some evil against which it exerts itself and which it can abolish; the expansive and liberating sense of relief experienced by a man who drinks when he is thirsty would not exist without the torment of thirst. We have heard it said that the boundless

71

happiness of Paradise is impossible since it would end in boredom for lack of contrast; it seems that in order to appreciate happiness there must be points of comparison and reference, and thus suffering. This view is erroneous for several reasons: in the first place, a man who is morally and intellectually unimpaired satisfies the need for contrasts or change by his discernment, detachment and discipline, and that is why he is never bored, unless someone bores him; in the second place, a superior man has the intuition of archetypes or essences and is kept in a state of supernatural equilibrium by the fact that his vision opens out onto the Infinite. In Paradise, nothing can fade, either objectively or subjectively, since things and perceptions are ceaselessly renewed through their contact with the Divine Infinitude; man thus finds himself freed, doubtless not from a certain need for compensating activities or rhythms, but from the psychological or moral necessity of contrasting changes. The metaphysical proof of this is the Divine Felicity itself, which does not suffer in the least from being without shadows, but which necessarily contains "dimensions" to the extent that it projects itself into the realm of *Māyā*, or to the extent that our way of envisaging the Divine Order is linked to this realm.

It is said that habit dulls the feelings, and this is true *de facto* but not *de jure*, for the psychological phenomenon of habit itself suffices to attest to a lack of gratitude and also of depth, at least on the plane of things that are supposed to make for happiness, but not on the plane of things we have to endure or that are a matter of indifference. From another angle, the stability of happiness depends — quite apart from any question of destiny — not only on the beauty and wisdom of our attitude but also, and above all, on an opening towards Heaven — as we have said — which confers upon the experience of happiness a life continually renewed. One must realize in earthly mode that which will be realized in heavenly mode; this is the very definition of nobility of character.

*

* *

There are two kinds of antinomy, one "vertical" and the other "horizontal," according to whether there is opposition or reciprocity: the relationship between positive and negative, real and illusory, good and evil pertains to vertical antinomy, and that between active and passive, dynamic and static, masculine and feminine, to horizontal antinomy. In other words, the positive pole is "above" and the negative pole is "below," whereas the active pole is "on the right" and the passive pole is "on the left." The opposition between a good and an evil, which is found in the peripheral regions of the cosmos, is excluded from the central region; the paradisal world contains only qualitative "horizontal" reciprocities, and its contraries are situated outside and beneath its domain.

We say "qualitative" because evil too has "horizontal" complementarities, since the active and passive poles are neutral in themselves and are asserted at all levels. As for the "vertical" relationship — the confrontation between positive and negative — it is universal in the sense that it represents a priori the gap between the Absolute and the relative; *Māyā* beginning in the Divine Order itself and bringing about the hypostatic degrees. Moreover, depending on our way of viewing things, "verticality" and "horizontality" are interchangeable, as we observed earlier: from a certain point of view, *Māyā* is the *Shakti* of *Ātmā* just as Infinitude is the complement of the Absolute, or as All-Possibility prolongs Necessary Being. From another point of view, *Māyā* is relativity or illusion, and is not "on the left" but "below." As the universal archetype of femininity, *Māyā* is both Eve and Mary: "psychic" and seductive woman, and "pneumatic" and liberating woman; descendent or ascendant, alienating or reintegrating genius. *Māyā* projects souls in order to be able to free them, and projects evil in order to be able to overcome it; or

73

again: on the one hand, She projects her veil in order to be able to manifest the potentialities of the Supreme Good; and, on the other, She veils good in order to be able to unveil it, and thus to manifest a further good: that of the prodigal son's return, or of Deliverance.

*

* *

It is worthwhile recalling here that Hindu doctrine accounts for the possibility of evil by means of the concept of the universal triad: *Sattva-Rajas-Tamas,* namely — analogically speaking — "luminosity," "heat," "darkness"; this last is not evil as such but its ontological root. In certain forms of symbolism — occasionally even in the Bible — there is nonetheless a coincidence *de facto* between the punitive and destructive function of God — personified in India as *Shiva*[10] — and the genius of evil, the Satan of the Semites; *Shiva* is in fact the Divine summit of *Tamas,* so to speak, but he is not of course "darkness," "heaviness" or "ignorance"; at most he comprises a negative or dark aspect from the world's point of view, precisely because he chastises and destroys. The confusion — real or apparent — between Divine Wrath and the genius of evil is an ellipsis which signifies that evil, insofar as it is a necessary phenomenon, is in the final analysis part of a celestial function.

On the one hand, God "loves" the world because the world manifests God;[11] but from another standpoint, God "punishes" the world because, in this regard, it is not its aspect of divine manifestation that is in question, but on the contrary its remoteness and "otherness" in relation to

10. This is then the particularized *Shiva* of the "Triple Manifestation" *(Trimūrti: Brahmā-Vishnu-Shiva),* and not the Supreme *Shiva* who is synonymous with *Parabrahmah* and thus possesses and controls all functions.

11. In creating the world, "God saw that it was good"; and He "made man in His image."

74

God. There is harmony on the one hand and opposition on the other between "Necessary Being" and "possible being"; all existence is an oscillation, contradictory on the surface, but basically homogeneous, between these two magnets that are moreover incommensurable. For this reason, man is the personification of an alternative whose dimensions escape his immediate vision. In other words, the very reason for being of the human condition is to choose, and to make the right choice: to opt for liberating participation in Necessary Being, and not for enslaving wandering through the labyrinth of the possible and in the direction of nothingness. And likewise, this is why every man is priest,[12] *pontifex,* "pontiff": the builder of the bridge between earth and Heaven, the bridge that leads from the present exile to the other shore; the shore of Peace close to the Immutable.[13]

As we have said, evil has no being in itself — it possesses it only on loan and in its neutral substance — whereas the Good is the being of all things; Being is thus synonymous with the Good, as certain Sufis have pointed out. Every man participates in Being through his existence and his faculties and carries it so to speak within himself; every man has within himself access to the Good and thus to Beatitude; "the Kingdom of God is within you."

It is true that owing to the "fall," this access has become dependent upon external conditions: the gateway of the human heart being closed, the gateway of the Celestial Heart has had to open, and has done so by means of Revelation and the Law; "without me ye can do nothing." But this transfer cannot prevent the Sovereign Good from

---

12. Which Islam intends to emphasize in restoring to man his primordial priestliness.

13. As the *Prājña-Paramitā-Hrdaya-Sūtra* enunciates it: "Gone, gone; gone towards the other shore; gone to the other shore; O Enlightenment be blessed!"

75

dwelling in our own heart and retaining all its freedom in relation to us; it is precisely in order to be able to act within us that it acts outside us. Man, marked by evil, bears in his quasi-transpersonal center the miracle of his salvation, whether he knows it or not, and whether he wishes it or not.

The Sovereign Good is both Omnipotence and Mercy; implacable Geometry and liberating Beauty.

Universal Eschatology

Eschatology is part of cosmology, and cosmology is a prolongation of metaphysics, which in turn is essentially the same as the *sophia perennis*. It may be asked by what right eschatology is part of this *sophia*, given that, epistemologically speaking, pure intellection does not seem to reveal our destinies beyond the grave, but rather universal principles. In reality, the knowledge of these destinies is accessible thanks to the knowledge of principles, or to their correct application. And in fact, it is not solely through the outward way of Revelation[1] that we can know the immortality of the soul but also by comprehending the profound nature of subjectivity; for to say total or central subjectivity — not partial and peripheral as in the case of animals — is to say capacity of objectivity, intuition of the Absolute, and immortality.[2] And to say that we are immortal means that we existed before our human birth — for what has no end cannot have a beginning — and in addition, that we are subject to cycles; life is a cycle, and our former existence also must have been a cycle in a chain of cycles. Our future existence may also proceed by cycles; at least it is condemned to this to the extent that we have not

1. Although Revelation always constitutes the occasional cause, or the initial cause, of the corresponding intellection.
2. As we have demonstrated on other occasions, above all in our book *From the Divine to the Human*, in the chapter "Consequences Flowing from the Mystery of Subjectivity."

77

been able to realize the reason for being of the human state which, being central, permits precisely of escaping the "round of existences."

The human condition is in fact the door towards Paradise: towards the cosmic Center which, while forming a part of the manifested Universe, is nonetheless situated — thanks to the magnetic proximity of the Divine Sun — beyond the rotation of the worlds and of destinies, and thereby beyond "transmigration." And it is for that reason that "human birth is hard to attain," according to a Hindu Text; in order to be convinced of this, it suffices to consider the incommensurability between the central point and the innumerable points of the periphery.

*

* *

There are souls who, fully or sufficiently conformed to the human vocation, enter directly into Paradise: they are either the saints or the sanctified. In the former case, they are great souls illuminated by the Divine Sun and dispensers of beneficent rays; in the latter case, they are souls who, having neither faults of character nor worldly tendencies, are free — or freed — from mortal sins, and sanctified by the supernatural action of the means of grace that they have made their viaticum. Between the saints and the sanctified there are doubtless intermediary possibilities, but God alone is the judge of their position and their rank.

Nevertheless, among the sanctified — those saved by sanctification both natural and supernatural[3] — there are those who are not perfect enough to enter directly into Paradise; thus they will await their maturity in a place which the theologians have termed an "honorable prison," but which in the opinion of the Amidists is more than that,

---

3. This is is not a contradiction, for the specific nature of man comprises by definition elements open to the supernatural.

since according to them this place is situated in Paradise itself; they compare it to a golden lotus bud which opens
when the soul is ripe. This state corresponds to the "limbo
of the fathers" *(limbus* = "edge") of the Catholic doctrine:
according to this very particular perspective, the just of
the "Old Covenant" found themselves in that limbo before
the "descent into the hells" of the Christ-Savior;[4] a conception above all symbolic and very simplifying but perfectly
adequate as to the principle, and even literally true in
cases which we need not define here, given the complexity
of the problem.

After the "lotus" we must consider "purgatory" properly so called. The soul faithful to its human vocation, that
is, sincere and persevering in its moral and spiritual duties, cannot fall into hell, but before entering Paradise it
may pass through that intermediary and painful state
which the Catholic doctrine terms "purgatory." It must
pass through purgatory if it has faults of character, or if it
has worldly tendencies, or if it is charged with a sin for
which it has not been able to compensate by its moral and
spiritual attitude or by the grace of a sacramental means.
According to Islamic doctrine "purgatory" is a transient
abode in hell: God saves from the fire "whomsoever He
wills," which is to say that He alone is the judge of the
imponderables of our nature; or in other words, He alone
knows what our fundamental possibility or our substance
is. If there are Christian denominations that deny purgatory, it is at root for the same reason: because the souls of
those who are not damned, and who *ipso facto* are destined
for salvation, are in the hands of God and are His concern
alone.

Regarding Paradise, it is necessary to take into account
its "horizontal" regions as well as its "vertical" degrees: the

---

4. All things considered, it is in this place that Dante places *de facto*
the sages and heroes of antiquity, even though he associates them with
the Inferno for theological reasons, since they were "heathens."

former correspond to circular sections, and the latter to concentric circles. The former separate the various religious or confessional worlds, and the latter the various degrees within each of these worlds. On the one hand, there is the *Brahma-Loka* of the Hindus, for example, which is a place of salvation like the Heaven of the Christians, although it does not coincide with it;[5] and on the other hand, within one and the same Paradise, the place of Beatitude of modest saints or of the "sanctified" is not the same as that of the great saints. "There are many rooms in my Father's mansion,"[6] and yet there are no impenetrable barriers between the various degrees, for the "communion of saints" forms part of Beatitude;[7] neither is there any need to maintain that there is no communication possible between the various religious sectors, at least on the esoteric plane where it can be meaningful.[8]

Before going further, and regarding eschatology in general, we would like to make the following remark: it has often been argued that neither Confucianism nor Shintoism explicitly admits the ideas of the Beyond and of immortality, but this is not quite so since they have the cult of ancestors; if there were no afterlife, this cult would be

5. Those Hindu Paradises from which one is expelled after the exhaustion of "good karma" are places, not of salvation but of transient reward; "peripheral" and not "central" places, and situated outside the human state since they pertain to transmigration.

6. This saying comprises also, and implicitly, an esoteric reference to the celestial sectors of the diverse religions.

7. And let us specify that, if there are degrees in Paradise, there are also rhythms, which the Koran expresses by saying that the blessed will have their nourishment "morning and evening." There is, moreover, no world without hierarchic levels of cycles, that is, without "space" or "time."

8. This possibility of interreligious communication is also clearly meaningful when one and the same personage, at once historical and celestial, appears in different religions, as is the case of the Biblical Prophets, even though their functions differ according to the religion in which they manifest themselves.

meaningless, and there would be no reason for an emperor of Japan to go and solemnly inform the souls of the deceased emperors of this or that event. Moreover it is known that one of the characteristics of shamanistic traditions is the parsimony — not the total absence — of eschatological information.

*

* *

We must now comment on the infernal possibility, which maintains the soul in the human state, and on the possibilities of "transmigration," which on the contrary cause the soul to leave the human state. Strictly speaking, hell too is a phase of transmigration, in the final analysis, but before releasing the soul towards other phases or other states, it imprisons it "perpetually," but not "eternally"; eternity pertains to God alone, and in a certain manner also to Paradise in virtue of a mystery of participation in the divine Immutability. Hell crystallizes a vertical fall; it is "invincible" because it lasts until the exhaustion of a certain cycle whose duration God alone knows. Those who enter hell are not those who have sinned accidentally, with their "husk" so to speak, but those who have sinned substantially or with their "kernel," and this is a distinction that may not be perceptible from without; they are in any case the proud, the wicked, the hypocrites, hence all those who are the opposite of the saints and the sanctified.

Exoterically speaking, man is damned because he does not accept a given Revelation, a given Truth, and does not obey a given Law; esoterically, he damns himself because he does not accept his own fundamental and primordial Nature which dictates a given knowledge and a given comportment.[9] Revelation is none other than the objective and

9. "God wrongeth not mankind in aught; but mankind wrong themselves." (Koran, Sura "Jonah," 44).

81

symbolic manifestation of the Light which man carries in himself, in the depths of his being; it reminds him of what he is, and of what he should be since he has forgotten what he is. If all human souls, before their creation, must attest that God is their Lord — according to the Koran[10] — it is because they know "preexistentially" what Being, the Truth and the Law are; fundamental sin is a suicide of the soul.

It remains for us to speak of another possibility of the afterlife, namely "transmigration,"[11] which lies totally outside the "sphere of interest" of Semitic monotheism, which is a kind of "nationalism of the human condition," and for this reason has in view only what concerns the human being as such. Outside the human state, and without speaking of angels and demons,[12] there remains, for this perspective, only a kind of nothingness; to be excluded from the human condition amounts, for monotheism, to damnation. However, between this way of looking at

10. "And (remember) when thy Lord brought forth from the Children of Adam, from their loins, their seed, and made them testify of themselves, (saying): Am I not your Lord? They said: Yea, verily. We testify. (That was) lest ye should say at the Day of Resurrection: Lo! of this we were unaware; Or lest ye should say: (It is) only (that) our fathers ascribed partners to God of old and we were (their) seed after them . . ." (Sura "The Heights," 172 and 173) — These preexistential creatures are the individual possibilities necessarily contained within All-Possibility, and called forth to Existence, not produced by a moral Will, but by the existentiating Radiation.

11. Not to be confused with metempsychosis, whereby psychic elements — perishable in principle — graft themselves upon the soul of a living person, which may give the illusion of a "reincarnation." The phenomenon is benefic or malefic according to whether the psychism is good or bad; that of a saint or that of a sinner.

12. Islam also acknowledges the *jinn*, the "spirits," such as the genii of the elements — gnomes, water-spirits, sylphs, salamanders — and other immaterial creatures, sometimes attached to mountains, caverns, trees, sometimes to sanctuaries. They intervene in white or black magic, thus either in therapeutic shamanism or in sorcery.

things and that of the transmigrationists — Hindus and
Buddhists especially — there is a point of juncture, and it
is the Catholic notion of the "limbo of infants" where infants who have died without baptism are supposed to
abide, without suffering; now this place, or this condition,
is none other than transmigration through worlds other
than our own and consequently through non-human
states, inferior or superior, as the case may be.[13] "For wide
is the gate, and broad is the way that leadeth to perdition,
and many there be which go in thereat": since, on the one
hand, Christ could not have wished to say that most men
go to hell, and since, on the other hand, "perdition" in
monotheistic and Semitic language also signifies leaving
the human state, one has to conclude that the saying
quoted concerns in fact the mass of the lukewarm and the
worldly, who are unaware of the love of God — including
those unbelievers who benefit from extenuating circumstances — and who deserve, if not hell, at least expulsion
from that privileged state which is man; privileged because giving immediate access to paradisal Immortality.
Incidentally, the "paganisms" offered access to the Elysian
Fields or to the Isles of the Blessed only to the initiates in
the Mysteries, not to the mass of the profane; and the case
of the "transmigrationist" religions is more or less similar.
The fact that transmigration, when starting from the human state, begins almost always with a kind of purgatory,

---

13. Either "peripheral" or "central": analogous to the state of animals in the first case, and to that of men in the second; the fact that
there is something absolute in the human state — as there is something
absolute in the geometric point — precludes the evolutionist and trans-
formist hypothesis. As with earthly creatures, angels also are either
"peripheral" or "central": either they personify a divine Quality, which
confers upon them both a given perfection and a given limitation, or
they reflect the divine Being Itself, in which case they are ultimately
one: it is the "Spirit of God," the celestial Logos, which polarizes into
Archangels and inspires the Prophets.

clearly reinforces the image of a "perdition," that is, of a definitive disgrace from the human point of view.

The baptism of newborn infants has the objective — aside from its intrinsic purpose — of saving them from this disgrace. As a result, in the event of death they remain in the human state, which in their case will be paradisal, so that this outcome, which the "nationalism of the human state" has in view, coincides with the celestial end that the sacrament has in view for adults. And it is with the same motive that Moslems pronounce the Testimony of Faith into the ear of the newborn, which evokes the whole mystery of the sacramental power of the *Mantra*. The intention is just the opposite in the very special case of the voluntary transmigration of the *bodhisattvas*, who pass only through "central" states, that is, those analogous to the human state; for the *bodhisattva* does not desire to stay in the "golden prison" of the human Paradise, but on the contrary seeks to radiate in non-human worlds until the end of the great cosmic cycle. This is a possibility which the monotheistic perspective excludes and which is even confined to *Mahāyāna* Buddhism, without for all that being obligatory for all Mahayanists, even if they be saints; the Amidists, in particular, aspire only to the Paradise of *Amitābha*, which practically is equivalent to the Hindu *Brahma-Loka* and to the Paradise of monotheistic religions, and which is considered not as a "celestial dead-end," if one may so express it, but quite on the contrary as a virtuality of *Nirvāna*.

We cannot pass over in silence another aspect of the problem of destinies beyond the grave; it is the following: theology — Islamic as well as Christian — teaches that the animals are included in the "resurrection of the flesh":[14] but whereas human beings are sent either to Paradise or

14. Bodily death and the subsequent separation of the body and the soul are the consequence of the fall of the first human couple; a provi-

to hell, animals will be reduced to dust, for they are not supposed to have an "immortal soul." This opinion is founded on the fact that the Intellect is not actualized in animals, whence the absence of the rational faculty and of language. But in reality, the infra-human situation of the animals could not mean that their subjectivity is not determined by the law of *karma* and thus engaged in the "wheel of births and deaths";[15] this law also concerns, not a given isolated plant, but the vegetable species, each of which corresponds to an individuality, although it is not always possible to distinguish between the limits of a species and groups which merely amount to modalities of it.

*

* *

We have distinguished five posthumous outcomes of earthly human life: Paradise, the limbo-lotus, purgatory, limbo-transmigration, hell. In the first three outcomes the human state is retained; in the fourth, it is left; in the fifth, it is retained only to leave it ultimately. Paradise and the lotus are beyond suffering; purgatory and hell are states of suffering in varying degrees; transmigration is

sional situation which will be rectified at the end of this cosmic cycle, except for some privileged beings — such as Enoch, Elijah, Christ, the Virgin — who mounted up to Heaven with their bodies "transfigured."

15. In Sufism, it is "unofficially" admitted that particularly blessed animals were able to follow their masters into Paradise, full as they were of a *barakah* of irresistible compulsion; which, all things considered, is not at all implausible. As for the question of knowing whether there are animals in Heaven, we cannot deny it, because the animal world, like the vegetable world which constitutes the Heavenly "Garden" (*Jannah*), is part of the natural human ambience. But neither the paradisal animals nor the plants of the "Garden" come from the earthly world; according to the Moslem theologians, the plants and animals of Heaven have been created then and there for the elect, which amounts to saying that they are of a quasi-angelic substance; "and God knoweth best."

not necessarily a suffering in the case of the *bodhisattvas,* but it is a mixture of pleasure and pain in the other cases. Or again: there are two places of waiting for Paradise, one gentle and one rigorous, namely the lotus and purgatory; and there are two exclusions from Paradise, also one gentle and the other rigorous, namely transmigration and hell; in both of these latter cases, the human condition is lost, either immediately as in the case of transmigration, or ultimately, as in that of hell. As for Paradise, it is the blessed summit of the human state, and strictly speaking it has no symmetrical opposite, despite certain simplifying schematizations having a moral purpose;[16] for the celestial world stems from the Absolute "by adoption," and the Absolute has no opposite, except in appearance.

Eternity belongs to God alone, as we have said; but we have also alluded to the fact that what is called "eternity" in the case of hell is not the same as in the case of Paradise, for there is no symmetry between these two orders, the one nourishing itself from the cosmic illusion and the other from the divine Proximity. Paradisal perpetuity is nonetheless relative by the very nature of things, in the sense that it opens onto the Apocatastasis, through which all positive phenomena return to their Archetypes *in divinis;* but in this there is no loss or privation, firstly because God never gives less than He promises or never promises more than He intends to give, and secondly — or rather above all — because of the divine Plenitude, which could not lack anything.

---

16. The cosmic "opposite" of Paradise is not only hell, but also transmigration, and this illustrates the transcendence and independence of Paradise. Let us add that there are *ahādīth* which testify to the disappearance — or the final vacuity — of hell; "watercress will spring up therein," the Prophet is supposed to have said, and also, that God will pardon the worst of sinners.

Considered from this point of view, Paradise is really eternal;[17] the end of the "manifested" and "extra-principial" world is a cessation only from the point of view of the limitations which produce manifestation, but not from that of intrinsic and total Reality, which on the contrary allows beings to become again "infinitely" what they are in their Archetypes and in their single Essence.

*
* *

All our preceding considerations may seem arbitrary and imaginative in the highest degree to one who clings to that immense simplification which is the scientistic perspective; however, they become plausible when on the one hand one acknowledges the authority of diverse traditional data — and we need not return here to the validity of this authority, which coincides with the very nature of the "naturally supernatural" phenomenon of Tradition in all its forms — and when on the other hand one knows how to draw from human subjectivity all the immediate and distant consequences it implies. It is precisely this subjectivity — this dazzlingly evident mystery — that modern philosophers, including the most pretentious psychologists, have never been able to grasp nor wished to grasp, and that is not surprising since it offers the key to metaphysical truths as well as mystical experiences, the one like the other requiring all that we are.

"Know thyself," said the inscription of the temple at Delphi;[18] and the same is also expressed by this *ḥadīth:* "Whoso knoweth his soul, knoweth his Lord"; and similarly the Veda: "That art thou"; namely *Ātmā,* the Self at

---

17. Which, moreover, is indicated in Sufism by the expression "Garden of the Essence," *Jannat adh-Dhāt;* this Garden divinely transcends the "Gardens of the Qualities," *Jannāt aṣ-Ṣifāt.*

18. Formulated by Thales, then commented upon by Socrates.

once transcendent and immanent, which projects itself into myriads of relative subjectivities undergoing cycles and determined by localizations, and which extend from the least flower to that direct divine Manifestation which is the *Avatāra*.

Part Two

The World of Tradition

The Mystery of the Hypostatic Face

In some Moslem authors one meets with the rather surprising opinion that no "Envoy" or founder of religion loved God as much as the Prophet of Islam did, and that none of them was as much loved by God as he. It will be said that this is a mere matter of prejudice, ignorance and lack of imagination; and this is true *de facto*, but it is not an exhaustive explanation, for the opinion under consideration benefits — as a religious sentiment or quasi-moral act — from a background which transcends the order of purely human options.

The key to the enigma is that there is not only a personal God — who is so to speak the "human" or "humanized Face" of the suprapersonal Divinity — but that there is also, "below" and resulting from this first hypostatic degree, what we may term the "confessional Face" of God: it is the Face that God turns towards a particular religion, the Gaze He casts upon it, and without which it could not even exist. In other words: the "human" or "personal Face" of God takes on diverse modes corresponding to so many religious, confessional or spiritual perspectives, so that it could be said that each religion has its God, without thereby denying that God is One and that this Unity can at any time pierce the veil of diversity. The fact that the God of Islam manifests, or can manifest, Himself differently from the God of Christianity, could not mean that Christians and Moslems do not in substance worship the same God.

91

The Divine Being contains all the spiritual possibilities and consequently all the religious and mystical archetypes; having projected them into existence, He looks upon each of them with a particular and appropriate Gaze; in an analogous sense, it is said that the angels speak to each person in the appropriate language. This "Gaze" or "Face" is a kind of new "divine subjectivity," subordinated to that of God as such, and transmitting it to man in a particular mode; it is thus that colorless light, without ceasing to be light, projects the colors of the rainbow; and it is thus that water, transformed into ice, gives rise to crystallizations and consequently to differentiated and even opposed manifestations. If there is a conflict between religions, confessions and ways, it is because there is competition between archetypes; these could never be fundamentally contradictory — the apparent opposition of the colors red and green is resolved precisely in their colorless origin — but they are nonetheless mutually exclusive, except at their centers, which by definition are non-formal and open onto pure light.

It is important to understand that the Hypostasis-"Face" or -"Gaze" is not an abstraction, but on the contrary a concrete divine self-determination — in view of a given singular or collective human receptacle — which projects into the human *Māyā* a whole particular universe with its own laws, possibilities and prodigies. In this sense, it can be said that to change one's religion is to change planets; and to understand a foreign religion as a phenomenon is above all to grasp that it is a planet and not simply a continent, even though there are of course degrees of remoteness or difference, hence in the feeling of estrangement that a foreign religious climate can inspire.

The sun is one, but it looks towards the planets with different gazes, so to speak, and it is seen differently according to their situations in space; this is perhaps a simplistic image, but it is in any case sufficiently adequate to illustrate the point.

92

*

* *

Exoterically it will be said — in Moslem language — that God sent Muhammad in order to found Islam; esoterically, it will be said that the archetype *in divinis* of the "Islamic possibility" projected this possibility into existence, and thereby became God for this projection. This projection is not separated from God as such, but "particularizes" Him in a certain fashion, while nonetheless communicating all the qualities and functions of God to the human receptacle; but it does this, precisely, in accordance with the "style" required by this particularization.

Each Divine Face operates by means of a Key Idea which describes it and which is everything: when one says "Christ," in Christian surroundings, one has said everything; the mystery of the saving manifestation takes precedence over everything else, there is only one decisive truth, namely that "God became man so that man might become God." Now the "hypostatic specification" — the "Divine Face" which projected into the world this particular aspect of the relationship "God-man" — in a sense takes upon itself the responsibility for all the consequences that the archetype provokes in the human world, not excluding the quite natural phenomenon of religious prejudice. However: even in this limitation, God does not cease being God — the only God there is — and He does not allow any one of His particular projections an absolute triumph. He contradicts it either *ab extra* or *ab intra*, that is, either by another religion, or by the *sophia perennis; spiritus autem ubi vult spirat.*

In the Moslem climate, the Key Idea — the ontologically indisputable Idea, so to speak — is the postulate of the One God; to say *Allāh* is to say everything; in a quasi-existential manner, this word closes the door to any dispute. And this quality of absoluteness redounds necessarily on the Messenger, and it is this which allows the assertion —

93

in good conscience and under the gaze of the corresponding "hypostatic Face"[1] — that no one was more loved by *Allāh* than the Messenger of *Allāh*, namely, the spokesman of the Key Idea that this Name expresses and manifests. This is an example of what we have more than once termed the "relatively absolute" — a paradoxical expression, to be sure, but indispensable on the plane of metaphysical analysis.[2]

More specifically, the Key Idea of Christianity is the dazzling phenomenon of the only man-God, who is unequalable and *a fortiori* unsurpassable, and alone capable of saving souls; for the Moslems, it is the fulgurant evidence of the Absolute, of the sole Principle, which is indivisible, inviolable and invincible. The certitude of the Absolute is absolute, as "the doctrine of Unity is unique" *(at-Tawḥīdu wāḥid);* and as faith in the Savior is salvific.

Each religion is a system which is not only dogmatic, mythological and methodical, but also cosmic and eschatological. One cannot measure the values of one system with the standards of another;[3] and this does not contradict the evident homogeneity of their common essence.

*

* *

1. In an implicitly conditional manner, however, since it is a "form."

2. The *Vedānta* distinguishes between the "non-supreme" Principle *(Apara-Brahma)* and the "supreme" Principle *(Para-Brahma);* the first is not, as is the second, the Absolute in itself, but it is "practically" the Absolute in relation to the world; it is thus "relatively absolute." The personal God is "absolute" without being intrinsically "the Absolute."

3. In an analogous manner, and on an entirely different plane, the values of one art cannot be measured with the standards of another; the values of Far Eastern music cannot be judged, for example, by the criteria of Western music; the needs and intentions are too different, even though the reason for being of art — as *a fortiori* of spiritual ways — is the passage from accidentality to the substance, or from the world of husks to that of the archetypes.

94

As a religion, Christianity is an *upāya* — a "saving strata-gem," hence one formal system among others — and the divinity of the Messenger does not change this fact; "God alone is good," said Christ. The limitation of the Christian system appears from the outset in its axiomatic definition of man as a "sinner" who can approach God only on this basis, hence the implicit or explicit rejection of all gnosis. But man is also the "child of God," God being the "Fa-ther," and moreover "my kingdom is not of this world"; all of which indicates an esoterism of love intended as such for a society of spiritual men, but not for a whole human-ity.[4] In fact, the legalistic application of this "wisdom of the saints" has created a dangerous scission in the social body, as is shown in Christian history by the underlying tension — or the chronic warfare — between the clergy and the laity, in the Catholic world above all.[5]

The "hypostatic Face" that presides over Islam "re-acted" against this perspective: not only against the dan-ger of scission and disequilibrium, but also and a priori against the idea that "man equals sinner" and against the idea that "God became man." This second idea deter-mined trinitarian theology or more exactly the equation between the aspect of trinity and the Absolute, whence a "Christocentrism" dominating everything *de facto*. On the one hand, Islam brought God back, so to speak, to His pri-mary meaning and to His transcendent essentiality, and

4. This society or this *civitas Dei*, was realized by Christianity in the monastic orders, at Mount Athos especially.

5. The Orthodox world was not able to resist this movement. Be that as it may: when one examines, image by image, the history of Euro-pean costumes — first the princely and then the bourgeois, both femi-nine and masculine — it is hard to believe that these are Christian cos-tumes, progressively marked as they are by worldliness — or even fri-volity — in short, by an almost total absence of the religious sense; one wonders how it is possible that these people read the Gospel, knew what a crucifix is, confessed and took communion.

on the other hand, it brought man back to primordial and "supernaturally natural" priesthood, thereby sacralizing the entire society.

For Islam, God is not the "Father" — at least not a priori and towards everyone — but rather the "Lord," which is more appropriate as regards an entire collectivity; as for man, he is the "slave" — not the "child," which for Moslem sentiment would presuppose a mystical intimacy — but he is also, thanks to his human dignity precisely, the "vicar" on earth, hence the representative of God. According to this perspective, the love of God is excellent to the extent that it is founded on the postulates of Islam; now God loves most perfectly the slave-vicar, the mirror of the divine Unity. Moslems cannot "reason" otherwise than within the framework of their system;[6] for them, Muhammad is pre-eminently the "servant" because he personifies — in accordance with the idea of "Lord" — the "prostration" of the creature, and he is also pre-eminently the "vicar" because he personifies a complete legislation and, on this basis, exercises the monarchic function, at once spiritual and temporal.[7]

God cannot contradict Himself, obviously, but He can manifest different dimensions of His one Substance, these dimensions being differentiated by *Māyā*. The Christian system, hostile to the "flesh," to "nature" and to the here-below, implacably excludes all sexual *yoga* or all "tantrism," whereas the Islamic system, being on the contrary favorable to the natural norm and to equilibrium,

---

6. One should not lose sight of the fact that Christ is a relatively esoteric phenomenon — hence his disdain for "prescriptions of men" and his insistence upon inwardness — and that exoteric Islam, legalistic by definition, could not do otherwise than to level a kind of reproach at him for this fact, at least indirectly. "Jesus was perfect — a dervish told us — but he was not able to prevent his being made a god."

7. Not to mention the specifically Islamic argument that the last of the "Envoys" must be the most eminent, because terminality rejoins primordiality while realizing an unprecedented synthesis.

tends to sacralize what nature, at once wise and generous, offers us; for man is there not only to master and transcend the particular facts — innocent in themselves — of his ambience and life, he is also there to ennoble and sanctify them, in short to integrate them into his "verticality," his vocation and way. There is not only a mysticism of sacrifice, there is also a mysticism of gratitude.

The hypostatic Faces of God "personify" diverse archetypes; hence the very notion of "love of God" is also affected and differentiated: sacrificial in the Christian perspective, this same love in the Islamic perspective intends to be more "inclusive," without thereby neglecting ascesis, since it is supposed to realize all the modes which existence itself grants us. It is necessary to take into account this play of the archetypes when one clashes with a confessional annexation, a priori of God Himself, and of the love of God. And it is necessary to understand that the hypostatic Face to which this annexation refers, necessarily stands surety for the opinions or sentiments conforming to the world of compossibles which It has created, even when this incidentally entails breaking the shell of the symbolism and manifesting — quite paradoxically — its quintessence which is the Truth of "everywhere and always."[8] Every religion comes from God and for that reason "commits" God — to some degree and in certain respects — within the framework of a particular belief, but this does not thereby make God in His aseity an adept of any given credo; *quod absit.*

It could also be said that on the plane of diversified Revelation, God operates by antinomism: He does not at the outset reveal the Truth in all its complexity, but successively or sporadically proposes antinomic aspects,[9] each of

---

8. Thus the Koran readily reminds us that "God doeth what He wills."

9. The role of antinomism — dialectic through contrasts — in diverse theologies, the Palamite theology especially, is well known. Theo-

which opens at its center onto the total Truth; and total Truth does not reveal itself in a gratuitous fashion, for it has its exigencies which in the final analysis engage all of man.

*

* *

Undeniably, the assertion — even if it be indirect — that there exists a religious Messenger more perfect than Christ, has something deeply shocking about it. But one must not lose sight of the fact that from the Moslem point of view, the assertion that Jesus is God in virtue of an intrinsic Trinity[10] — so that in a certain fashion God is Jesus — is at least as shocking, outside its point of view, as the preceding opinion is. And similarly: for a Hindu or a Buddhist, the assertion that their respective Revelations are merely "human" or "natural" in origin, that they are in no way "supernatural," and that Christianity alone can save man — this assertion or this opinion, is for them just as odious as the underestimation of Christ is to the Christians.[11] Similarly again, it is deeply odious to Jews — and also to Moslems — to hear that an Enoch, a Noah, an Abraham, a Moses, an Elias, had access to Paradise only thanks to the mediation of Jesus of Nazareth; whereas they would accept in principle the intervention of a Divine

logians propose two apparently irreconcilable enunciations whose very contradiction provokes — like a spark flashing from flint — an illuminative, if not always expressible, intuition.

10. That is: not to say Trinity is not to say God.

11. This underestimation can extend to the Mother of Christ: when the Koran declares that "God hath chosen thee (O Mary) and hath purified thee, and hath raised thee above all women," there are commentators who find a way of having it say merely that Mary was "the most pious woman of her time," no more, no less; an absurd minimalizing which is explainable by the fear of mariolatry; it is always a case of *ad majorem Dei gloriam*, which in the climate of a sensitive monotheism is theologically and psychologically decisive.

Power — the "Divine Names" amounting practically to hypostases — hence of an intemporal and transhistorical Logos.[12]

All things considered, the idea that a particular religious Messenger could have loved God more perfectly than another given Messenger, or than all the others, seems to us to be a rather unnecessary luxury. In Islam — where it has come from even one of the most eminent writers — it follows neither from the Koran nor from the Sunna; thus it is nothing more than pious excess. The question remains whether in a religious space such initiatives or deviations can be avoided, and to what extent they can be avoided, given that religion lives — humanly speaking — in part from enthusiasm and that no one can impose boundaries on the overflowings of faith, or even on theological or mystical speculation, as the case may be.

For us, what counts is to know, not only why extreme opinions — whatever their level — exist in religious climates, but also why they are met with even among esoterists of the highest rank. Doubtless one has to take into account here an element of *bhakti*, of mystical love, that embraces everything in a single flow of devotion without troubling itself with a critical sense which, in such climates, appears as a dissonance and almost as a betrayal. The mythical garden of tradition is a closed and blessed system from which the contemplative does not willingly depart in order to become involved in the cold and neutral space of an "exact science," such as "comparative religion". If the gnostic sees himself obliged to transcend the world of forms, he will do so preferably through the prov-

---

12. Which Christ personified in fact. Islam recognizes this in naming Jesus the "Spirit of God" *(Rūh Allāh)*, but without drawing the same consequences as Christianity. Moreover, we contest, not that Christ "descended into hell" to raise souls to the "beatific vision," but that this saving gesture could concern without distinction all men of good will — even outside Israel — who lived prior to the Christian era.

idential opening situated at the very center of his own garden; he will hesitate — in a narrowly confessional climate — to penetrate into the stratosphere of Truth pure and simple. This does not prevent a less affective and more objective outlook from maintaining all its rights, and this is so *a fortiori* on the universal plane whereon the great initiates intend to be situated, and where they are situated to the extent that they possess sufficient information;[13] the exact knowledge of phenomena certainly is not detrimental to the profound knowledge of God.

In summary, we shall say that there are two "extenuating circumstances" for the extreme opinions to be met with in confessional climates: the first, just spoken of, is a devotional mentality favoring a thought that is more pious than correct; the second, set forth before, is the irresistible evidence — and the invincible power — of the Key-Idea. In the wake of this Idea, or in the shadow of this Divine "Face," excessively unilateral or even exorbitant opinions benefit at least from a certain plausibility, either formal or implicit: either they are admissible in a very particular respect, or they express truths independently of their literal meaning. In any case, it is best to regard them as symbols — unless they are intrinsically aberrant — and not view them outside the Idea which determines them directly or

---

13. One Sufi cheerfully advises his prince to oppress the Christians — which after all goes a bit far — while another on the contrary frequents them and tends to protect them; which proves that in a climate at once esoteric and traditionally rigorous, there is a margin that allows of very different options. Let us note in this connection that the oppressive anti-Christian laws of the Ummayyad caliph Omar II are sometimes attributed, either through ignorance or fraudulently, to the great Omar, the companion of the Prophet and second caliph, whose magnanimity towards Christians was well known. Be that as it may: in many cases one could apply to the disproportion between the absolute Idea and the relative opinions — including symbolic yet ill-sounding legends — the following verse of the Koran: "Say *Allāh!* Then leave them to their vain talk." (Sura "Cattle," 91).

indirectly, and which, if it cannot always justify or corroborate them without reservations, can at least excuse them; this Key-Idea which projects the Absolute into the human *Māyā*, and which in the religious space is everything.

Outline of Religious Typologies

The Absolute[1] can be approached in two ways, one founded upon "God as such," and the other founded upon "God become man"; this is what distinguishes between Abrahamism, Mosaism, Islam, Platonism, Vedantism on the one hand, and Christianity, Ramaism, Krishnaism, Amidism, and in a certain sense even Buddhism as a whole, on the other.

The second of these ways — that of the Logos — is comparable to a boat which takes us to the other shore: the distant land makes itself near through the form of the boat; God becomes man because we are men; He holds out His hand by assuming our own form. This implies, firstly that man cannot save himself otherwise than by this hand held out by God, and secondly, that the image of "God as such" becomes blurred in the mythology and saving economy of "God become man."

The first of these two ways, on the contrary, is founded upon the idea that man has access to God by his very nature — fallen or not — and that it is faith in "God as such" that saves. But this faith must be integral, it must encompass all that we are, namely thought, will, activity, senti-

---

1. Even if it be the "relative Absolute," since all of the Divine Order is absolute with respect to human relativity, although not with respect to the pure Intellect, which transcends all relativity — effectively or potentially — otherwise we would not even have the notion of the Absolute.

103

ment; and this is what Sacred Laws intend to realize, for the collectivity as well as for the individual.[2] Man is saved by conforming himself perfectly to his theomorphic nature; the Sacred Law is what we are, essentially and hence primordially.

*

* *

It is in the nature of things that neither of these two fundamental ways can completely exclude the truth of the other; the way of the Logos must find a secondary place — if only symbolically — within the framework of the way of "God as such," and conversely. Shiism, with its quasi-divinization of Ali and Fatimah and its subsequent imamolatry, projects the Christian perspective, so to speak, into Islam; Amidism, with its saving trust in the Mercy of the Buddha-God Amida, seems to introduce this same fundamental perspective into Buddhism.[3] Hinduism — as could be expected — contains both perspectives, the one alongside the other, it is Krishnaite as well as Vedantic.

But the extreme examples of Shiism and Amidism are insufficient, for it is a question of recognizing the foreign perspective not only within a given particularist crystallization, but also and even above all in the general religion:

---

2. From the point of view of the Law, what conforms to virtue is not only what serves the spiritual and possibly also the material interest of the individual and his immediate neighbor — spiritual interest being unconditional and material interest conditional — but also what serves the equilibrium of society; whereas from the point of view of the simple nature of things, that is in conformity with virtue which is just in itself — without regard to the needs of the collectivity — and which therefore serves a given spiritual interest, on condition of not harming the legitimate interests of anyone.

3. Whereas in both cases, the possibility of Christian influences has to be totally discarded. It is a question of spiritual archetypes, not of historical phenomena.

thus, the cult of the Logos is found in Islam generally in the attenuated, and as it were neutralized, form of the mystical cult of Muhammad, the canonical expression of which is the "Blessing of the Prophet." The cult of the Logos is also found in Buddhism generally, in the form of the quasi-adoration of the Buddha, of which the classical image of the Buddha is the best known sign.

Clearly, the inverse reverberation also exists, and is manifested quite paradoxically by the fact that the religions of the "Logos become man" view him to a certain extent as if he were "God as such": they too aim at realizing what is integrally and primordially human through recourse to a Law, but starting from the idea of a "Word made flesh" and of the fundamental incapacity of man marked by the fall; thus without leaving their general and determining outlook.

The confrontation between the two types of religion, one centered on God-as-such and the other on God-become-man, evokes the principle of dual relationship, not only between man and God, but also between wife and husband, the people and the monarch, and other complementarities of the kind. If in confronting religions, we have shown that there is an access to God that is direct and another that is indirect, we could say as much of purely human situations: the wife can be subordinate to the husband only on condition of being his friend on another plane, namely that of their common humanity; similarly, an elementary rule of monarchy is that if on the one hand the monarch must rule his subjects, on the other hand he must always preserve towards them a relationship of man to man, as is shown by the examples of the great kings of the past.

For the Westerner, access to the personality of the Prophet is as if blocked by the following factors: the language of the Prophet, at first sight strangely that of the "average man," even "earthbound" and somewhat "discontinuous"; then a certain complication and quasi-

105

accidentality of his private life; and above all, the canonical claim placing him above Christ. Thus, access to the personality of the Prophet — barring the case of a conversion pure and simple, the result of which will be the forgetting or the incomprehension of the personality of Jesus — this access, we say, is only possible by a metaphysical or esoteric detour that grasps the phenomenon from within and proceeds from synthesis to analysis, from the essence to the form, or from the substance to the accident. We have dealt with this on other occasions and we confine ourselves here to the following observation, which will appear a priori as a begging of the question — but this is of little importance since the spiritual, religious, cultural and historical consequences of the Muhammadan phenomenon prove its legitimacy, efficaciousness and grandeur: whereas Christ passes through the human state only reluctantly so to speak, and finds himself therein almost as a stranger, the Prophet has both feet in the human condition and thereby accepts and realizes to perfection all that is positively human and natural; he is deliberately cut off from the Divine Order — for the divine Intention of Islam wills the Messenger to be "man, whole man and nothing but man" — and this, for the Christian, blurs the traces of his sanctity. The Prophet has essentially the sense of society, whereas Christ has in view only man as such; thus Saint Paul, while aware of the social usefulness of marriage, seems to wish to make it a kind of punishment, as if to take vengeance upon the man who has not chosen celibacy in view of the Holy Spirit, and despite the sacramentalization[4] of marriage which refers to the Holy Spirit and entreats its participation. Be that as it may, the dogmatic formulations and the ethical stipulations necessarily have something harsh about them, if one may put it thus; a religion is not built with nuances.

---

4. Which in this context amounts to an expedient.

However strange the following assertion may seem — and in the case of Christ this would be devoid of meaning — Muhammad is the Prophet of what is "reasonable"; of a reasonableness that is not mediocre, of course, but made of psychological and social realism, and thus capable of being a support for the path of ascension. On occasion, but not rarely, the Prophet could also be as "piously unreasonable" as the Christian ascetics, and it is to these atypical examples that the esoteric asceticism mentioned earlier refers; atypical, because these examples are foreign — if not contrary — to the principle of measure and equilibrium of the common religion.

The Prophet, say the Sufis, realizes the synthesis of all spiritual possibilities, whereas each of the other Messengers represents only one of these possibilities, or at least stresses only one. Whereas the message of "inwardness" or of "essentiality" of Jesus — opposed to the cult of "outer observances" — is univocal and arresting, it is precisely the character of synthesis or equilibrium of the Muhammadan message which renders the spiritual portrait of the Prophet more or less "imprecise," at least when seen from without and in the absence of the necessary keys. For the Moslems, however, this same portrait is perfectly intelligible, for they conceive him a priori as embodying the whole range of greatness and beauty, not on the basis of an abstraction, of course, but by following the complex itinerary of the great and small incidents that mark the life of the hero. It could be said that in a certain sense the Islamic perspective, as regards both the Messenger and the spiritual life, goes from analysis to synthesis, whereas the Christian perspective on the contrary proceeds from synthesis to analysis, in both respects.

A symbolical truth is not always literal, but a literal truth is necessarily always symbolical. The various Islamic traditions concerning Christ, the Virgin and the Christians, are certainly not to be taken literally — which does not invalidate their intentions or their symbolism — but when Islam teaches that there is, and has always been, the possibility of salvation outside the person of Christ, and that he is but one saving manifestation among others — which does not mean that he is the same as the others — it speaks the literal truth, at least in this particular respect.[5] Jesus is exclusively "the Door" and "the Way," assuredly, but the Door, or the Way, is not exclusively Jesus; the Logos is God, but God is not the Logos. The whole question is to what extent we accept this axiom and what consequences we draw from it.

From an altogether different point of view, there is no religion that does not comprise elements comparable in practice to what, in Zen, is called a *koan:* namely a logically vexing formula, meant to burst the shell of the mind, not from below, of course, but from above; and in this sense all religion, in this or that aspect or detail, is a "divine folly," but is compensated a priori by the dazzling and quasi-existential evidentness of its message as a whole. The skeptic or the pedant may well clash against inevitable contradictions, but there will always be a fundamental element in religion that allows him no excuse, but that, on the contrary, furnishes a largely sufficient excuse for the contradictions of the religious symbolism.

*

*   *

After all of these considerations concerning a question of religious typology, and concerning in the final analysis the enigmas of dogmatic language in general, we believe we can change the subject within the framework of this same chapter, and broach a related problem, that of the relationship — or of certain relationships — between the

---

5. But not in respect of the characteristic and truly unique modality realized by the "Word made flesh"; although the Koran acknowledges that Christ is "Spirit of God" and that he was born of a Virgin.

Christian West and the Moslem East; we say "broach," for it is not a question of treating the problem in depth. First of all, we must point out the following phenomenon: it too often happens that Westerners who are more or less close to Islam accuse other Westerners of misunderstanding it and of maintaining unpardonable prejudices with regard to it, instead of studying it with love. This is perfectly unjust and even properly absurd, for even aside from all possible prejudices — and Westerners are certainly not the only ones who have them — it is a fact that Islam rejects the dogmas of Christianity, puts the Koran in place of the Gospel, the Prophet in place of Christ, and believes that the Christian religion ought to give way to the Moslem religion; and these opinions largely suffice to render Islam unacceptable and even hateful in the eyes of the Christians. What matters from the point of view of total truth — as we have said and now repeat — is to know that the anti-Christian theses of Islam fundamentally have only a symbolic, extrinsic and "strategic" meaning resulting from a positive spiritual intention which obviously is unrelated to historical phenomena. The same remark applies, *mutatis mutandis*, to Christian theses seeking to invalidate all other religions, and so on. God has undoubtedly willed different and divergent religious worlds to coexist on the same planet; He does not ask that within any one of these worlds the others be taken into account. It is after all with the same "existential logic" that each individual believes himself to be "I." If God wills that there be diverse religions, He cannot wish that a given religion be some other religion, each must therefore have solid boundaries.

Under normal conditions, the Moslem has only one religion which envelopes and penetrates him to the point that it is impossible for him to leave it, except by apostasy. This truism seems astonishing, but its function can be seen immediately if we add that the average Christian, on the contrary, seems to have practically three religions at once, first Christianity, then "civilization," and finally his "country" or "nation," or "society," or some other political ideology, according to the fluctuations of fashion or according to the surroundings; religion properly so called is put into a corner, human reflexes are compartmentalized.[6] One of the causes of this phenomenon is an inveterate taste for novelty, notorious already in the Greeks, starting with the so-called classical age, and no less so in the Celts and the Germans; whence a tendency to changefulness and thus to infidelity, or even to Luciferian adventure; a tendency neutralized, it is true, by more than a millennium of Christianity. Quite paradoxically, one cause of this cultural incoherence — an indirect cause no doubt, but combining in the long run with the cause already pointed out — lies within the religion itself, namely the fact that the doctrine and the means of Christianity surpass the psychological possibilities of the majority, and give rise to a secular scission between the religious domain which tends to keep men in a kind of sacred ghetto, and the "world" with its seductive invitations — irresistible for Westerners — to philosophic, scientific, artistic and other adventures progressively detached from religion, and in the end turning against it.

Islam, it will be said, is sterile, and crushes all creative initiative. Perhaps, but it does so "deliberately" and with good reason; for thereby it has been able to maintain a Biblical world for a millennium and a half in the face of a West ever more Promethean and dangerously "civilized." No doubt, Islam has not been able to escape the decadence that has invaded, with rare exceptions, all of the East — a passive decadence so to speak, which the West

---

6. In this, the East has finally rejoined the West, sometimes with the zeal of a "sorcerer's apprentice." As regards the general degeneration of humanity, it has been foreseen by all the traditions, and it would be paradoxical, to say the least, to deny it in the East in the name of traditionalism.

has not undergone, occupied as it has been with its active and creative deviation. Nonetheless, Islam has protected the East for several centuries against the civilizationist virus, whose expansion it has considerably retarded and whose effects it even more or less cushioned in a preventive manner.[7] The West, for its part, has been able to maintain, within the very framework of its deviation and independently of it, human qualities which in the East have been seriously encroached upon — not everywhere but in too many sectors — to the point that certain Western judgements benefit at least from extenuating circumstances; the feelings of superiority of the colonizers were not always entirely gratuitous,[8] as the defenders of the East — as enthusiastic as they are abstract — like to think.

No doubt the Luciferian abuse of the intelligence which turns against truth, and finally against man, is worse than mere moral decay; but the surprising facility with which the decadent East makes common cause with Western modernism as soon as it is able to, proves that between both excesses there is something like a providential complementarity, and that moral decay, after a certain point, is far less innocent from the spiritual point of view, and therefore from the point of view of truth, than one would have believed at first sight; or that one would have

---

7. A phenomenon which must be pointed out here in order to forestall the most unfortunate confusions, is the false traditionalism which makes of Islam the standard-bearer of an ultra-modern and subversive nationalism by introducing into the religious formalism ideas and tendencies that are at the antipodes of Islamic doctrine and the Moslem mentality. Analogous enterprises have seen the light of day in other traditional worlds.

8. Modernist Orientals acknowledge it more or less, but hold the tradition responsible for it, and it is moreover in virtue of their modernism that they have an interest in acknowledging it. They even go so far as to reproach colonialism for having maintained traditional institutions.

liked to believe out of love for tradition.[9] Besides, to actually adhere to tradition is to adhere to it with discernment
and not through simple routine. To lack discernment to
the point of deserting tradition as soon as political conditions permit or invite doing so — or to accept this deser-
tion without protest[10] — is not really to have a traditional
mind, and does not testify to a mentality worthy of being
cited as an example or of being admired without reservation.

In a general way, one of the most disappointing discov-
eries of our century is the fact that the average believers,
no matter where, are no longer believers; that they do not
truly have a sensibility conformed to their religion, and
that one can tell them anything. Humanity is steeped in
the *kali-yuga*, the "iron age," and most men are beneath
their religion — if they still have one — to the point of not
being able to represent it consciously and firmly; thus it
would be naive to believe that they incarnate a given traditional world, that is, that they are what this world is. To
the question of knowing whether the everyday East is still
traditional, one could answer yes and no; one cannot,
knowingly, answer simply yes, but no doubt it would be
even more inadequate to answer simply no, given the
complexity of the problem. All this is unrelated to reli-

9. Although one can accuse the West with spreading its errors
throughout the world, nonetheless there has to be someone to accept
them. Theology has never exculpated Adam, even though it was Eve
who was the instigator.

10. In certain cases, one has to take into account the fact that it is
necessarily anti-traditional men who dispose of the technical means
and above all of the arms, so that the traditional men are defenseless;
but in most cases this general situation would not prevent the partisans
of tradition from manifesting their resistance. We have been told more
than once, in the East, that all that has occurred is "willed by God";
now, one could, in analogous situations, as well have made use of this
reasoning since the Middle Ages and even since Antiquity, but no one
dreamt of doing so before this second half of the twentieth century.

gious typology, of which we have spoken at the beginning of this chapter; but since evil proceeds from excess as well as from privation — and the falsification of the good entails both faults[11] — the formal features of a religion necessarily influence the genesis of a given particular degeneration, albeit quite indirectly and by subversion. And this is observable in Eastern decadence as well as in Western deviation.

What fundamentally characterizes this deviation, which the simple word "materialism" cannot define, is a triple abuse of the intelligence: philosophic, artistic and scientific. It is from this Luciferism — inaugurated by "classical" Greece, then neutralized by a millennium of Christianity, and finally reinstated by the Renaissance — that the modern world is born. Moreover, it has ceased being uniquely Western, and this is not the fault of the Westerners alone.

Quite obviously, there is everywhere a decisive difference between spiritual men and worldly men, or between traditional and antitraditional men, the orthodox and the heterodox; but there is none, from the point of view of human values taken as a whole, between the East and the West. If a priori the West needs the traditional East, the latter has need a posteriori of the West which has been schooled by it.

11. Falsification results from the sin of pride; to falsify a good is to appropriate it for oneself, to subordinate it to an end which is contrary to it, thus to vitiate it by an inferior intention. Pride, like hypocrisy which accompanies it, can produce only falsification.

113

Two Esoterisms

The word "esoterism" suggests in the first place an idea of complementarity, of a "half" as it were: esoterism is the complement of exoterism, it is the "spirit" which completes the "letter". Where there is a truth of Revelation, hence of formal and theological truth, there must also be a truth of intellection, hence of non-formal and metaphysical truth; not legalistic or obligatory truth, but truth that stems from the nature of things, and which is also vocational since not every man grasps this nature.

But in fact this second truth exists independently of the first; hence it is not, in its intrinsic reality, a complement or a half; it is so only extrinsically and as it were "accidentally." This means that the word "esoterism" designates not only the total truth inasmuch as it is "colored" by entering a system of partial truth, but also the total truth as such, which is colorless. This distinction is not a mere theoretical luxury; on the contrary, it implies extremely important consequences.

Thus esoterism as such is metaphysics, to which is necessarily joined an appropriate method of realization. But the esoterism of a particular religion — of a particular exoterism precisely — tends to adapt itself to this religion and thereby enter into theological, psychological and legalistic meanders foreign to its nature, while preserving in its secret center its authentic and plenary nature, but for which it would not be what it is.

*
* *

115

The monotheistic Scriptures each manifest an *upāya*, a religious perspective — by definition particular and limiting — and more often than not hermeneutics is affected by it; such is not the case, however, for the fundamental formulations — or fundamental symbols — of the religions, which in themselves are not restrictive in any way.

In Christianity, the patristic formula of saving reciprocity is a priceless jewel: "God became man that man might become God"; it is a revelation in the full sense, of the same rank as Scripture, which may seem surprising, but which is a "paracletic" possibility, examples of which can be found — very rarely, it is true — in all traditional worlds. The saying *"anā'l-Ḥaqq"* of Al-Hallaj is a case of this kind, it is so to speak the Sufic equivalent of the Vedic *Aham Brahmāsmi*. Al-Hallaj himself affirmed this possibility of post-Koranic sayings situated at the level of the Koran, for which other Sufis did not pardon him, at least not in his time.

In Islam, the *Shahādah* — the affirmation of Unity in the form of the *yin-yang*, if we may say so, and "the most precious thing that I have brought to the world," according to the Prophet — expresses essential metaphysics in a way that comprises no confessional limitation; in Hindu terms, we could say that it is the equivalent at once of an *Upanishad* and of a *mantra*. The same is true for the second *Shahādah*, which attests to the mission of the Prophet and thereby evokes the mystery of immanence; it joins this mystery to the mystery of transcendence, indicated by the first *Shahādah*, at least a priori, for the first *Shahādah* also contains an "immanentist" meaning.[1]

---

1. We interpret the words "immanent," "immanence" and "immanentism" according to the etymological meaning: *immanens* means "dwelling within." The modern philosophical interpretation, starting with Spinoza, is abusive; immanence is neither identity, nor negation of transcendence; nor epistemological subjectivism, of course.

But there are not only formulas, there are also human theophanies. Christ, as universal symbol, and from the point of view of esoteric application, represents first of all the Logos in itself and then the immanent Intellect — *aliquid est in anima quod est increatum et increabile* — that both illuminates and liberates; the Virgin Mary personifies the soul in a state of sanctifying grace, or this grace itself. There is no theophany that is not prefigured in the very constitution of the human being, made as it is "in the image of God"; and esoterism aims at actualizing what is divine in this mirror of God that is man. Meister Eckhart spoke of immanent sacraments; symbols that are "congenial" can be supports, he said, no less so than the sacraments in the proper sense of the word.

Thus it is necessary to distinguish — we repeat — between an esoterism more or less largely based upon a particular theology and linked to speculations offered to us *de facto* by traditional sources — and it goes without saying that these doctrines or insights can be of the greatest interest — and another esoterism springing from the truly crucial elements of the religion and also, for that very reason, from the simple nature of things; the two dimensions can be combined, it is true, and most often do combine in fact. To be concrete: Christian esoterism is *de facto* Clement of Alexandria, Origen, Dionysius the Areopagite, Meister Eckhart, without forgetting Boehme and his school;[2] but it is also, and even above all and *de jure*, the universal truths — and the corresponding attitudes — which issue from the doctrinal, ritual and "phenomenological" foundations of Christianity.

As regards hermeneutics, which plays such an important role in Semitic monotheist esoterism, respect for

---

2. And without forgetting more particularly the esoterisms of pre-Christian origin, such as Hermeticism and the craft initiations; or chivalry, whose origin, however, seems uncertain to us.

given authors or accomplished "facts" must not allow us to forget that this science is supposed to proceed according to strict rules; Ghazali and others insist upon this. But it is far from the case that this principle has always been followed in a climate of religious and mystical enthusiasm; abuses of interpretation can be encountered even in an Ibn Arabi and even in the Zohar, most often owing to an insufficiently contained *bhakti*. In this domain there are three modes or degrees to be distinguished: firstly, an interpretation that springs harmoniously from a given symbolism; secondly, an interpretation that imposes upon the literal meaning a heterogeneous symbolism that this meaning could not possibly imply; thirdly, an interpretation contrary to the literal meaning, and this in virtue of the idea that every word of God, even if it is negative, allows of a positive interpretation; something which, in the opinion not only of the ulamas, but also of many esoterists, constitutes a flagrant abuse and a kind of pious perversion.

But let us return to the subject at hand: unquestionably, *Advaita-Vedānta* is an intrinsic esoterism, and as such suffices unto itself; but it is not an esoterism-complement, that is, an esoterism found alongside a religious system of a sentimental character. This is not to say that its situation within the economy of the spiritual means of Hinduism is one of complete isolation. Beside it there is in fact the bhaktic *Vedānta* of Ramanuja, which corresponds to a religious mysticism in the sense that it is based upon a conception of the personal God; consequently it is dualistic and voluntaristic, like the Semitic spiritualities in their general manifestation. But the advaitists are the first to acknowledge that *bhakti* corresponds to a degree of the one truth, hence to a necessity, and that it is legitimate for that very reason.

*

* *

Strict and universal esoterism — of the "advaitic" type so to speak — has necessarily always existed in the climate of Semitic monotheism, and this opinion can be supported by the following arguments. Firstly, if in every religious climate such an esoterism is necessarily to be found, it is for the simple reason that everywhere there are men whose nature requires it; namely, men whose intelligence, discernment and contemplativeness are proportionate to pure metaphysics and thus to the corresponding path. Secondly, if there are no documents proving the more or less traditional existence of this gnosis, that is because it was of necessity transmitted orally — apart from certain providential exceptions which are also necessary — given that gnosis is independent of the exoteric systems which may be its vehicle, and that therefore it inevitably comprises aspects that are incompatible with them.

Thus it is not surprising that from the strictly theological point of view, gnosis is the "enemy number one." By its recourse to intellection it seems to make Revelation redundant and even superfluous, which in theological language is called "submitting Revelation to the judgement of reason"; this confusion — which is not disinterested — between reason and intellection is altogether typical. Plato's anticipated retort is the following, and it is all the more justified in that religious sentimentalism has had extremely serious, if providential, consequences since "it must needs be that offenses come": "All force of reasoning must be enlisted to oppose anyone who tries to maintain an assertion and at the same time destroys knowledge, understanding and intelligence." *(Sophist,* 249).

Fideist mentalities readily make the point that pure intellectuality — which they confuse with the most profane philosophy since they conceive only of reason — has as its goal and result only "speculations" and "theses," things purely "natural," whereas religion alone, according to them, offers "life" and the "supernatural." This is a per-

119

fect begging of the question, and it is to hold that "life" and the "supernatural" are obtained only outside intelligence; in the final analysis it is to deny that man — who alone is gifted with an intelligence capable of absoluteness — is "made in the image of God."

*

* *

The rationalistic pseudo-gnosis of our times appears as the repercussion of the theological antignosis of the first centuries; and this vengeful effect of a distant cause comes not only from without, from the unbelieving world, but is produced in the very bosom of the Church. In fact, two causes combine here: hatred of gnosis, on the one hand, and thirst for novelty and need for change on the other; these are the typical features of the creative and adventurous, and in its extreme effects even Luciferian, mentality of the West. This mentality has combined, both providentially and unfortunately, with what we may term Christian "innovationism," and, more indirectly, even with Jewish messianism.

Be that as it may, it is neither metaphysical discernment nor contemplativeness that is primarily lacking in the Europeans, but rather a sense of the static, of the principle of immutability, in short, of the "immovable mover". The "worldliness" of Westerners lies in their inventive hypertrophy — the Westerner always feels the need to "burn what he has worshiped" — and in their cultural changefulness; whereas the "worldliness" of Easterners lies only in the excessiveness of the ordinary passions of body and soul, which is bad enough when it is recalled that passions becloud the intelligence, whatever the ethnic climate in which they arise and whatever the natural gifts of a particular individual or collectivity.

The point will perhaps be made that lack of the sense of the Immutable or of appreciation for static values or functions proves a corresponding lack of a metaphysical men-

120

tality. This is true for the majority — in a necessarily relative manner — but it in no wise excludes the presence of metaphysics and contemplativeness; it would be abusive therefore to conclude that in these respects the West has nothing and has everything to learn from the East. It would indeed be in the greatest interest of the elite of the West to draw inspiration from the Vedantic doctrine and to assimilate thoroughly the key notion of *Māyā in divinis,* even though this notion is to be found in a Meister Eckhart and doubtless also in others, in a more or less incidental manner; but finally, intellectuality does not depend entirely upon this notion, as is proved by Thomism and by Vaishnavite *Vedānta. Grosso modo,* the West possesses all that is essential, but does not wish to hear of it, and in this consists its drama and absurdity.

Deficiencies in the World of Faith

One may be astonished and even scandalized at the frequency, in religious climates, of more or less unintelligent opinions and attitudes, let it be said without euphemism. The indirect cause of this phenomenon is that religion, the goal of which is to save the largest possible number of souls and not to satisfy the need for causal explanations of an intellectual elite, has no reason for directly addressing the intelligence as such. In conformity with its end and with the capacity of the majority, the religious message is basically addressed to intuition, sentiment and imagination, and then to the will and to reason to the extent that the human condition requires it; it informs men of the reality of God, of the immortality of the soul and of their ensuing consequences for man, and it offers man the means of saving himself. It is not, does not wish to be, and cannot be or offer anything else, at least not explicitly; for implicitly it offers everything.

In other words: religion addresses itself a priori to what is capable of "stirring" to action the will of the average man; it could not address the intelligence in an immediate manner, for, precisely, it is not the intelligence that gives impetus — spiritually and eschatologically speaking — to the average or ordinary man, thus to the majority. Consequently, religion "acts" as if intelligence could never determine the spiritual will; whence its distrust, and even hostility, towards "philosophers" or, what amounts to the same thing, towards the so-called "natural" intelligence.

123

A certain exclusion of the intelligence may already be noted at the scriptural level, not in the sense that the Scriptures could lack intelligence, *quod absit,* but in the sense that they occasionally use arguments which, being addressed to a given basically passional disposition, ignore intelligence in view of an efficacy that does not involve it; this attitude is by necessity accentuated at levels below Revelation, until it reaches the point of giving free rein to a moralistic opportunism which does not necessarily coincide with truth pure and simple, to say the least. In the Scriptures, intelligence — or what appeals to it — is found primarily in the symbolism, which offers all that the loftiest minds could need; this is so first of all because of the divine origin of Scripture and secondly because of the absolute exigency of religion. In other words, God never gives less than He promises, and He never promises more than what He actually gives.

As for pure metaphysics — and we need not insist at length here on the fact that it is necessarily found in the dogmas themselves inasmuch as they are universal symbols — it could never have the concrete and efficacious character of a message for the average man, even if he could mentally grasp certain of its elements; it is addressed directly only to those whose intelligence possesses a quality at once discriminative, contemplative and operative. Discriminative: that is to say, capable of discerning intuitively between the Absolute and the relative, and of prolonging this discernment onto planes that are relative; contemplative: that is to say, capable of attaching itself — in a "naturally supernatural" manner — to the consciousness of pure Being and to the pure Essence; operative: that is to say, predisposed to pass from potentiality to act, hence from the abstract to the concrete and from intelligence to will. These gifts are not necessarily absent in a specifically exoteric or religious climate, of course, but they are necessarily limited therein by reason of the primacy, in such a climate, of the formal and legislating Rev-

124

elation to the detriment of supra-formal and immanent Intellection.

Religion addresses itself to men as being capable of faith; it addresses itself in a direct manner to will and love — not to the intellect — and requires men to believe, love and act. We insist upon this so that a spiritual seeker, in reading religious books, may not become shocked when finding in them opinions or images that are excessive to the point of absurdity. Quite paradoxically, in traditional climates there is a certain right to pious extravagance, and it is better to know this in advance, in spite of those traditionalists who believe that everything traditional is sublime,[1] and who are sometimes but little removed from confusing confessional fanaticism with intrinsic "orthodoxy" and spiritual "authenticity."

Be that as it may, in order to account for a certain "lack of intelligence" in the religious climate, it is not enough to say that the majority of people are not metaphysicians in the strict sense of the word; all the more so since there are men who, while not being metaphysicians or "pneumatics," are endowed with perfect objectivity, that is, with a discerning, incorruptible, and impartial intelligence. What one should say is that the majority is much less than simply non-metaphysical, that they really have little intelligence, as the history of the world demonstrates to repletion, and as is proven by mundanity in all its forms.

*

* *

The reader will have understood that our intention is not to maintain that the world of faith lacks intelligence; it could not, since faith is a fundamental human phenomenon and moreover, and above all, since it aspires to the celestial and the eternal; but faith — and we are speaking here

---

1. "All that is national is ours," as the Duke of Orleans said.

of faith as simple belief and not as theological virtue and sanctifying charisma[2] — aspires to it in a self-interested and volitional manner, and not as the result of a disinterested perception of the nature of things; such intellectual perception would be unable to penetrate the hearts of the majority, given the passional nature of most of the men who live in the "Iron Age."

Confessional perspectives have a tendency to put form, which is particular, above essence, which is universal, and moral concern, which is self-seeking, above truth — in itself amoral — which is disinterested; it is as if the particular color of a lantern were to be taken for light itself on account of its luminosity. And one may say without exaggeration that for the confessionalists, sentimentality — pious prejudice — enters into the arsenal of intellectual means to such an extent that moralistic suspicion has practically the function of a doctrinal argument; it is not enough that the error attributed rightly or wrongly to the adversary be false,[3] it must be *ipso facto* immoral, and its cause must reside in its author. Moralistic prejudice here combines with confessional prejudice; the true and the false become practically synonymous with the moral and the immoral, which may be justified in certain specific cases, but not in all.

Justified in certain specific cases, we have said: for one has to be on guard against falling into the opposite error. The fact that some people unjustly attribute a theological opinion to a psychological cause, more particularly to a moral vice, cannot alter the fact that many philosophies "according to the flesh" have such a vice as their starting

---

2. Without belief, the spiritual way would lack a framework; but what produces holiness is faith, in the Pauline and mystical sense.

3. Moreover one has to distinguish between honorable and dishonorable errors; to speak well of someone through an error of judgement is not the same thing as to speak ill of someone mistakenly; but it is all too often the same thing for the theologians.

126

point, circumstances aiding. All too often, errors are simply what their author is, neither more nor less.

*

* *

Perhaps we may be allowed, by way of example, to introduce a digression, which on account of its content will lead us away from our subject, but which nonetheless refers to it through its psychological context. The bitter controversies which arose in the 5th century concerning the question of the two natures of Christ are well known: whereas for the official Church — the schism was not yet an accomplished fact — the two natures, human and divine, are united in the person of the "Word made flesh," for Nestorius they are definitely separated, so that Mary is the "Mother of Jesus" but not the "Mother of God"; for Eutyches on the contrary, Christ has only a divine nature, the human nature being no more than an appearance. What we wish to draw attention to here is not so much these doctrines as the way they were anathematized by Rome: according to Pope Leo I, Nestorius and Eutyches were necessarily impious people; in his Sermon XCVI, he speaks of the "wickedness of the heretics," of the "perfidious attacks of wolves and brigands," of their intention to "lead other people to perdition" after having themselves "followed the lies of Satan," and so on. Which is to say that men who — out of piety and zeal, obviously — have theological opinions other than Rome, can only have them through Satan and can only be, like him, wicked and perfidious; they can only be enemies of God and the Church. All this is pious and zealous — neither more nor less so than the opinions of Nestorius and Eutyches — but it is certainly not intelligent, if by intelligence one understands adequation to realities.

For after all, each of the two extreme opinions at issue here can be upheld, in a relative fashion: the first because it is eager to extol the glory of the transcendent God — we

127

do not see anything satanic in this intention, any more than in the fundamental tendency of Judaism and Islam — and the second because it is on the contrary eager to extol the divinity of Christ. These opinions may be somewhat excessive, but they certainly have nothing perfidious or demoniacal about them. One should not forget, moreover, that theological differences were not fundamentally abnormal in the 5th century; even a St. Thomas, much later, could venture to deny the Immaculate Conception, and it was not until the 20th century that the Assumption was established as a dogma. Nestorius' protest against the expression *Mater Dei* can be defended seriously and honestly; there is no doubt that this expression — which we accept as an ellipsis based on a perspective that is relative, to be sure, but nevertheless efficacious within its framework — unquestionably entails a certain "neutralization" of the perspective of transcendence to which Nestorius had a sacred right to be deeply attached.[4] In an analogous manner, the reduction — on the part of the Monophysites — of Christ's humanity to his divinity, is one of the possible consequences contained in the Christian perspective; it is in any case — like the Nestorian thesis — an aspect of Christ, which can and even had to assert itself under certain circumstances. As for the authors of these theses, we do not know whether they were saints or not, but they may have been, and it is even likely that they were.[5]

Here one could make the following objection: if, for a theologian given to abrupt alternatives, only the providen-

---

4. Without wishing to be disobliging, one may speak of a "Christianization" of God — in the case of the Trinity presented as the Absolute Reality — just as, in the case of Judaism, one may speak of an "Isrealization" of God. A simple question of *upāya* or *darshana*.

5. While many heresies of Antiquity have disappeared, the Nestorian and Monophysite churches still exist fifteen centuries after the ferocious anathematization of their founders.

tially normative doctrine can proceed from the Holy Spirit, from whom then, if not from the demon, can the divergent theses come? We may answer "from the soul," because it is proper to distinguish between an inspiration which is satanic and another which is simply natural and psychic. But this answer, though it has the merit of taking account of a real distinction, fails to take account of the following two factors: firstly, that a natural inspiration runs the great risk of being exploited by the Enemy if the contents of the inspiration lend themselves to it; secondly, that in cases like those of Nestorius and Eutyches, inspiration is not simply natural, nor *a fortiori* satanic; it is what we will call "archetypal," which is to say that, while not proceeding from the paracletic intention governing all providential orthodoxy, it nonetheless comes from the Holy Spirit as such to the extent that it manifests a plausible aspect of a spiritual or divine reality.

*
* *

Pious myopia is a phenomenon of little consequence in certain cases and of the greatest consequence in others; what is certain is that we meet with this flaw in all religious climates, because man is everywhere man, and the same causes always produce the same effects in the same circumstances, whatever the mode or degree of the phenomenon may be. After all, there is not only mental stupidity, there is also institutional stupidity, which clearly pertains to the order of the "precepts of men." To give only one example — chosen deliberately from outside the Bible — we may mention in this connection the "defilement" that the Brahman is supposed to contract from the shadow of a *shūdra* or an outcaste. The more or less pharisaical defenders of tradition will no doubt tell us that it is necessary to exaggerate in order to be able to maintain for thousands of years a traditional principle which in itself is plausible — namely the integrity of the Brahman caste —

129

and this can in fact be maintained. But the theory is one thing and the practice another, for one has to take account of modalities that the theory cannot always foresee. A "preventive war" can be justified, because the end can justify the means, but the means can also compromise the end; everything has its limits, and one runs the risk of curing the disease by killing the patient. Thus it is not surprising that Islam had so much success in India; that it could spread simply by persuasion and by contagion, without any participation of the Arabs.

These considerations concerning a particular kind of absurdity make us think, by association of ideas, of human stupidity in itself, not that of man as such — because not every man is stupid — but of the majority in all climates. Can one imagine anything more stupid than the anger or grief of an individual whose wife has given birth to a daughter, when he had hoped to have a son? Yet this is a usual occurrence among many peoples, in the past as well as today; the fact that economic or political considerations can come into play does not make this attitude any more intelligent or more noble. Many analogous examples of stupidities that have become customary could be cited; not to speak — in a much more pretentious order — of philosophy and "culture" in general, which are in fact the favorite terrains of the most glaring stupidity, but this applies to the modern world rather than to humanity as such. Be that as it may, religion is obliged to address men as they are, the men of all times; it has no choice. Two mysteries are combined in this fatality: that of Mercy and that of the absurd.

Some people consider that religion should be adapted to the "men of our times," which is disproportionate to say the least, for religion addresses man as such and not this or that man.[6] Doubtless, one must give modern man cer-

6. To man as such: that is, to every man. Not to this or that man: not to this or that contingent or even artificial category of men. The fact

tain additional explanations, since new errors — and new experiences — require new arguments; but to explain religion is one thing, and to dismantle religion under the pretext of explaining it, is another. Here is where essential esoterism could and should intervene; but in accordance with the law of gravitation and the line of least resistance what are preferred are new solutions that lead downwards; to crown it all, what is adopted are certain more or less extrinsic esoteric positions, plainly rendered inoperative in the absence of their fundamental context.[7]

Three notions largely lacking in what we may call the "world of faith" are the following: firstly, that of universal "Relativity" *(Māyā);* secondly, that of the "point of view" of the knower; and thirdly, that of the "aspect" of the known. It is definitely not a matter of falling into an integral relativism and denying the existence of intrinsic heresies, which indeed must be condemned unconditionally. The fact is, relative heresies — efficacious within certain limits — exist, and strictly speaking religion itself exhibits this character in relation to total Truth; and this is precisely what is expressed by the Buddhist term *upāya,* which could be translated as "spiritual stratagem" *(Kunstgriff* in German) or as "redemptory mirage." No doubt, the perspective of faith alone cannot — without contradicting itself — admit "points of view" and "aspects," any more

that a religion addresses a priori a given sector of humanity is not an objection here, all the more so since there is nothing absolute about this restriction.

7. To recognize the validity of all religions is certainly a commendable attitude, on the condition that it is not in the name of a psychological philosophy which reduces the supernatural to the natural; on the condition also that pseudo-religions and pseudo-spiritualities be excluded, something which a certain "ecumenicism" seems not to be aware of. Universalism is neither "humanism" nor a philosophy of indifference.

131

than it can admit the "relativity" of the hypostases or of creative Being;[8] everything in this perspective has to be absolute, on pain of losing the percussive force proportionate to the sensibility of the average man.

True, the perspective of faith does not necessarily imply a principial misunderstanding of intelligence, but it nonetheless gives a more limited idea of intelligence — one has but to think of Thomistic sensationalism — which inevitably opens the door to the abuses of sentimentalism, and at the same time explains or corroborates the compensatory necessity of an esoteric dimension. When this dimension is lacking, it is the profane philosophers who take over, to the great detriment of the whole civilization; because reasoning, as we have said more than once, is inoperative in the absence of pure intellection, at least on the plane envisaged here. What all rationalists alike ignore is that on this plane reason essentially needs information coming either from "Heaven" or from the "Heart"; information whose origin is thus either external or internal, the first being more often than not the occasional cause of the second, which indicates that in fact gnosis cannot do without Revelation;[9] *a posteriori* and in another connection, Revelation, inasmuch as it is "letter," cannot do without gnosis.

The rationalist reaction, while sometimes justified in its details, is all the more futile in that on the whole it replaces a believing unintelligence by an unbelieving unintelligence, which finally is much more pernicious since it is deprived of all that is essential; for it is useless to have a rigorously logical knowledge of a paving stone when one is ignorant of where the street leads; it would be much better to ignore the pavement, and to know the goal. This

8. Which a Meister Eckhart perceived perfectly.

9. It would be futile to believe that Plato drew everything from himself, or that a Shankara had no need of the *Upanishads*, although in principle such a thing is not inconceivable.

132

means that there is an intelligence which is ignorant and stupid through being ignorant of its ignorance; and it is certainly not this purely mechanical intelligence that we would justify against religious naivety: the latter knows at least where it is going, which from the human point of view is everything.

Nevertheless, our conclusion will not be that pious naivety — or else pious stupidity — is always excusable; while it is inevitable inasmuch as it is a possibility, it is not necessarily so in a given manifestation; thus we can abolish a given evil, but not evil as such. There is the play of *Māyā* and there is Providence; the history of the Church and that of the world testify to it. We can blame the shortcomings, but we will not dispute with what "is written."

There are many things that could be said about the multiple relations between knowledge and faith, or between intelligence and fervor; for example, that the Semites have excelled in the latter, and the Aryans in the former; all the same, they both needed each other — at least in the West — as in the story of the blind man and the lame man.[10] All told, the three Monotheisms could not get along without the intellectuality of the Greeks, and Europe in turn had the greatest need of the Semitic gift of faith. Bhaktic India and devotional Buddhism are far from being unaware of this vivifying and redemptory faith; as a dimension of the Heart-Intellect, faith, which then coincides with love, combines with gnosis in the depths of our being.

---

10. Scholasticism was an initial attempt — partially successful — to rehabilitate intellectuality; later came the Renaissance, a profane and Luciferian reaction, despite certain small islands of Platonism and esoterism. Baroque art signified a monstrous alliance between the abuse of intelligence and pious stupidity; the latter could celebrate orgies thanks to acquisitions from an ever more sterile Renaissance. What the baroque style proves in any case, is that an "intelligent" stupidity is a hundred times worse than a naive stupidity, that of the Madonnas of peasant origin for example.

133

World of faith, world of gnosis: these two meet in Beauty, which is the "splendor of the True," and which reconciles — beneath the mantle of the Holy Virgin — all the antagonisms that the spiritual aspirations of man can assume.

Confessional Speculation: Intentions and Impasses

The fact that both confessional opinions and the perennial Wisdom refer, in their substance, to the same transcendent order, enables us to broach them without leaving the framework of our general subject; and if there is an interest in broaching opinions that are doubtful, even on their own ground, it is for the simple reason that to rectify an error is to manifest a truth. This is moreover a dialectical means found in many Eastern and Western doctrinal expositions, from the pen of an Ashari as well as that of a Saint Thomas; which means that we are not innovating in this respect.

An initial question we wish to consider here is the following: many theologians of Islam, and not the least of them, consider that God wills evil because, they say, if He did not will it, evil would not occur; for if God did not will evil and it occurred nonetheless, God would be weak or powerless; now God is all-powerful. These thinkers are obviously unaware of the distinction, on the one hand, between "evil as such" and "such and such an evil," and on the other hand, between the subjectivity of the Divine Essence and that of the Divine Person: for the Divine Person is all-powerful in regard to the world, but not in regard to His own Essence; the former cannot prevent what the latter demands, namely the cosmogonic Radiation and the consequences it entails, which are: remoteness, differentiation, contrast and, in the final analysis, the phenomenon of evil. This amounts to saying — we repeat — that God has power over a given evil, but not over evil as such. If it be objected, with Ashari, that in that case God would be "weak" or "powerless," our reply is that this is in no wise an objection, and for two reasons: firstly, because a metaphysical limitation — with the impossibilities that it entails — is neither "weakness" nor "powerlessness" in the human sense of these words,[1] and secondly because in this case it is precisely a question of what is metaphysically impossible in relation to the God-Person; and it cannot be stressed enough that this is because the Omnipotence of the Divine Person bears on universal Manifestation only and in no way on the roots *in divinis* of this Manifestation, nor on the principial consequences of these roots, such as evil. According to a particularly ill-sounding and in fact blasphemous error, God does not "will" that we sin since He forbids sin, but at the same time He "wills" particular men to sin, for otherwise they would not sin;[2] an error which involves God's Subjectivity as well as His Will. In fact, evil springs from All-Possibility as "possibility of the impossible," or as "possibility of nothingness": privation of being is clad, quite paradoxically, with a kind of being, and this in virtue of the limitlessness of divine Possibility; but "God" cannot "will" evil as such.

Contrary to the Koran, which declares more than once that "God breaketh not pledges" *(lā yukhlifu 'l-mi'ād)* or "His promise" *(wa'dahu),* some exegetes insist on the idea

---

1. One may in certain cases reproach the weak for not being strong, but one cannot without absurdity reproach the relative for not being absolute; an ontological mode is not a moral blemish.

2. The Christian expression that "God permits evil," and that He does so "in view of a greater good" — despite the fact that His ways may not be comprehensible to us — such expressions may be morally satisfying without always being intellectually sufficient. Let it be noted that in Islam it is sometimes specified that God "inciteth to error" not in an active manner, but "by abandoning" man, or "by turning away" from him.

that God owes nothing to man, that He is absolutely free in regard to him, that He owes him no reckoning. In this pious concern to attribute to God an independence pushed to absurdity, they destroy the notion of man as well as that of God, and they forget that God created man because He desired the existence of a being to whom He could owe something, as is implied by the expression "created in His image." Moreover, if God desires something, He does so in conformity with His Nature, and this nature coincides with His Will while not being its product; which is to say that His Will results from His Nature and not conversely. The zealots of "Divine Right" could not be unaware of this, but they do not draw the consequences whenever they think they have to defend God's liberty, or His sublimity or His royalty. Let us specify that these zealots are not altogether blameworthy in attributing to God an unlimited moral independence, but this kind of independence belongs to the Essence, to Beyond-Being — which precisely does not legislate — and not to Being which creates, legislates and exacts retribution; thus not to the personal God. The confusion comes from the fact that theology — lacking the notion of *Māyā* — does not make an effective distinction between the hypostatic degrees in the Divine Order, concerned as it is with "unity" at all costs; not to mention the anthropomorphism which attributes to God a practically human subjectivity.

The dilemma of the exoterisms in monotheistic climates is on the whole the following: either God is One, in which case He is unjust — *quod absit* — and it is necessary to veil this apparent injustice either by a declaration of incompetence or by a reference to mystery, or again by a pious absurdity; or God is just, in which case His subjectivity is complex notwithstanding His simplicity, and despite the dogma of Unity, and it becomes necessary to veil this complexity by the same stratagems. In reality, intrinsic unity does not preclude extrinsic diversity which, moreover, is necessary since the world exists. And intrinsic justice does not preclude an appearance of injustice or at least of contradiction, this appearance being inevitable because of the complexity of the Divine Order, precisely; and the reason for this complexity is the existentiating tendency and the fact that existence cannot but comprise antinomies. On the one hand, the complexity of the Divine Order prefigures the diversity and antinomies of the cosmic order; on the other hand, these antinomies reflect in their way the complexity — conditioned by *Māyā* — of the Divine Order; thus the latter is partially encompassed within the principle of Relativity, so that only the Essence remains absolutely unengaged in the universal round. Exoterism cannot help attributing this glory of the Essence to the divine *Māyā* — that is, to all that it terms "God" — whence its difficulties and embarrassments; piety compels to a simplifying sublimism at the expense of coherence.

In any case, if out of concern for dogmatic coherence one seeks to maintain the unity of the Divine Subject — which clearly is legitimate from the point of view of the Divine Nature as such — one is then obliged to acknowledge different modes within the Will of the One God: namely a will that is active and direct and another that is passive and indirect, so to speak. This is to distinguish between what God "wills" in view of an immediate or at least foreseeable good, and what He "permits" in function of a principial necessity, the end of which is necessarily a "greater good," due to the nature of the Divine, precisely. Of course, the total mechanism of this "permission" most often escapes human imagination, in which case only details are grasped; but it is nonetheless graspable by the intelligence, and this is enough. Intellectual capacity is measured, not only by the quality, but also by the limits of its need for logical explanation, on condition of course that these limits be determined by this quality.

*
* *

"God alone is the Agent," since it is He who "creates" the actions of men. Well and good. But if it is a mistake to believe that it is we who act — as certain Sufis would have it — it is equally a mistake to believe that it is we who exist; if human action is in reality divine Action, then the human "I" is in reality the divine "I." If man "acquires" the act that in reality belongs to God, as Ashari teaches, then he also "acquires" the ego that in reality belongs to God; and one would like to know wherein lies the error or sin here: in the injustice of the action, as common sense would have it, or in the idea that "it is I who act," or again, in the "acquisition" of an act "created" by the unique Lord, as some Sufi or some theologian would have it. If there is illusion, it lies not in our conviction that it is we who act, but in our very existence,[3] for which we are obviously not morally responsible. If it is we who exist, it is also we who act. Since we exist, we are free; our acts are those of God only to the extent that, metaphysically, we do not exist, because He alone is.

If God has given men the conviction of being the authors of their actions, it is certainly not — as some Sufi has imagined — to prevent them from accusing God of being the creator of their sins; it is solely because once man exists he is *ipso facto* the author of his good or bad actions, which have the same reality or unreality as his existence, as we have said above. The concrete consciousness that God is metaphysically the underlying Agent is realizable only in virtue of the moral quality, or the ontological rectitude, as it were, of our actions;[4] it is a priori this rectitude

3. "There is no greater sin than existence," according to a formula as audacious as it is elliptical, attributed to Rabi'ah Adawiyah; and according to another formula of this kind, God alone has the right to say "I," and the sin of *Iblīs* was precisely to attribute this right to himself.

4. It is a question of intrinsic morality, conformed to the nature of things, whether or not it coincides with a given formal and institutional morality.

we must be concerned with and not the idea that it is God alone who acts. God did not delude us in creating us, and He did not delude us further in our conviction that we act freely. True, God is the source of our capacity to think and act, just as He is the source of our existence, but He cannot be the author responsible for our moral acts,[5] otherwise we would be nothing and He would be man.

It goes without saying that the underlying divine Activity is the same in good and bad actions, insofar as it is a question of activity as such. This reservation means that good actions, aside from their prefiguration in the divine Activity, first of all conform to the Sovereign Good — which is the substance of this Activity — and secondly are necessary for the release of the divine Agent in the soul, precisely because they conform to the *Agathón*, to the divine Perfection which is the reason for the existence of Activity as such.

Thus it is improper to say, without adding the indispensable nuance, that God is the Agent of our actions. However, if we say that "God alone is the Knower," having in mind metaphysical Knowledge as such — and not its reflection in the mind — we speak truly, for this Knowledge does not stem from specifically human subjectivity; it pertains to the "Holy Spirit," and it is what links us to the Divine Order, without for all that divinizing us; without this

5. If the Koran specifies that *"Allāh* hath created ye, ye and all that ye do," it is not with the intention of relieving man of moral responsibility but to point out the total ontological dependence of creatures; the proof of this is that in the same Koran God prescribes and forbids, promises and threatens, which is meaningful only in view of a responsibility other than His own. On the one hand, the Koran declares that "God inciteth to error whom He wills," — it should not be forgotten that, according to the Bible, God "hardened the heart of Pharaoh" — and on the other hand, the Koran specifies that "God wisheth them no harm, but it is they who harm themselves," and other expressions of the kind.

Knowledge or without its virtuality, man would not be man. The human being, by his nature, is condemned to the supernatural.

*

* *

"Therefore hath he mercy on whom he will have mercy, and whom he will he hardeneth. Thou wilt say then unto me, Why doth he yet find fault? For who hath resisted his will? Nay but, O man, who art thou that repliest against God? Shall the thing formed say to him that formed it, Why hast thou made me thus? Hath not the potter power over the clay, of the same lump to make one vessel unto honour, and another unto dishonour?" *(Romans*, IX, 18-21).[6] This passage enunciates an idea that is also found in Islam: God possesses all rights, not because He is holy or because He is the Sovereign Good, but because He is all-powerful; doubtless an argument of the conqueror and of the monarch,[7] which closes the discussion at the outset but explains nothing from the metaphysical point of view which, precisely, the Apostle did not wish to broach. Going to the root of the matter, one could obviously reply that man has a right to the need for logical causal explanations, a need that God has conferred upon him, and all the more so in that the question at hand is bound to arise; and it should not be forgotten that a simple question is not necessarily a "dispute." Basically, the Apostle's dismissal of our need for such explanations and of our common sense signifies that his intention is to veil the complexity of

6. "Surely your turning of things upside down shall be esteemed as the potter's clay: for shall the work say of him that made it, He made me not? or shall the thing framed say of him that framed it, He had no understanding?" *(Isaiah*, XXIX, 16). This voluntarist and fideist logic necessarily has in its context its reason for being.

7. At the level of sacred history, of course, but the psychology in question nonetheless keeps its specific character.

the Divine Order so as to safeguard the anthropomorphic image of the monotheist God. But more profoundly it is also a dismissal of the absurd question: why is a given possibility possible?[8]

Be that as it may, according to the Pauline doctrine, evil is necessary for the manifestation of the "Glory" of God: the "vessels of Wrath," namely those creatures destined for chastisement, are there to permit the appearance of the divine Quality of Wrath or Justice. This means that the sin to be punished, or the disequilibrium to be rectified, is the complementary negative aspect, or the providential support, of that divine Quality, which could not radiate without the concurrence of such occasional causes as the negative possibilities which are necessarily included in the Infinitude of the Principle. But there is also the following to be considered: a man of good will would not dream of asking God: "Why hast Thou made me pious and honest?" any more than the hardened sinner would ask: "Why hast Thou made me a sinner?" For the man of good will has no reason to complain, and as for the sinner, if he found a reason for asking his question — if he suffered from being a sinner — he would sin no longer, for nothing obliges man to sin. The question: "Why hast Thou made me thus?" has meaning only for an irremediable situation. Now it is not the state of being a sinner that is irremediable, it is the deliberate, hence prideful, will to sin; and no one can deny that man does what he wills. Certainly, this does not take away the right of a bad man logically to ask the question at hand, but it does forbid him to ask it morally, since he desires to be what he is.

The problem of predestination is resolved metaphysically by the doctrine of Possibility: everything possible is obviously "identical to itself," it "wills" to be what it is, on-

---

8. The same remark is true for the Koranic expression: "He createth what He wills" (*yakhluqu mā yashā'*).

tologically and initially;[9] it is not the personal, creating and legislating God who "wills" evil, He simply transfers into Existence the differentiated and differentiating possibilities which reside in the All-Possibility of the divine Essence, of which He, the personal God, is but the first Hypostasis. As for man, we could say that "damnation" is as it were the passive side of the substantially perverse individual, he whose very substance is sinful, the active side being sin, precisely; willing evil — willing it in his very substance — this individual "condemns" himself, whereas sin "through accident," hence exterior to the individual substance, leads merely to "purgatory."[10] Let it be noted that "mortal sin" resides not in the act alone — a temporal fact cannot entail for the agent an intemporal consequence — but resides above all in the character, hence in the substance, which means that one and the same act may have an import that is either accidental or substantial, depending upon whether it results from the shell or the kernel of the person. When man improves his character, *Deo juvante,* God no longer takes into account past sins whose roots have disappeared from the soul: a sin which one would no longer commit is a sin effaced, whereas man must pay for an old transgression which he could still commit. It goes without saying that what is at issue in all

9. This is what the Koran expresses by these terms: "But if they (the damned) were to be brought back (to Earth), they would return to what had been forbidden them. . ." (Sura "The Troops," 28).

10. In Christianity, theology is indecisive as regards predestination, not in itself, but as regards God's intention, which according to some is independent of human merits, and according to others is more or less dependent upon them, at least in certain cases; but it is the first of these opinions, upheld by Saint Augustine and Saint Thomas, which has prevailed in the end, or has predominated over the others. The Catholics blame the Protestants for being certain of their salvation; aside from the fact that the majority of Catholics, ignorant of theology, have no other attitude, this certitude is actually an element that is more methodic than dogmatic — at least in pious people — and it curiously rejoins the analogous certitude of the Amidists.

this is not that which appears as sin by its form, but that which is sin on account of an intrinsic blemish, for the worth of an act lies in its intention.

*

* *

According to Christ, it is necessary that "the Scriptures be fulfilled"; and the Koran speaks likewise of a "Book" in which the smallest facts are written down in advance, and also of a "Guarded Tablet" on which the future is inscribed, or rather all that is possible and all that will be realized. This Divine Book is none other than All-Possibility, at various degrees: firstly, it is the Infinite itself, which pertains to the Essence or to Beyond-Being, the dictates of which Being — the personal God — cannot but accept; secondly, it is Infinitude insofar as it belongs to Being, in which case it is All-Possibility, not at the purely principial and potential level, but at the archetypal and virtual level; thirdly, it is the limitlessness of Existence, thus All-Possibility manifesting and manifested, or in other words the Logos projecting the possibilities and the world that realizes them.

We have said that God cannot but accept the dictates of the Essence; nonetheless, being the personal God, He cannot will all evils in a positive and explicit manner; but He wills, and "must will" by His very nature, that "the Scriptures be fulfilled," and He can still determine modalities. Another mystery is the relativity of certain possibilities inscribed in the "Book," namely things that must be in an absolute manner, and things that may not be, at least as regards their mode and which consequently may change form or level; otherwise it would be useless to ask favors of God, and the Islamic custom of asking God, during a night of Ramadan, to change into good the evil that is inscribed on the "Guarded Tablet," would have no meaning. God is sovereignly free, which implies that there is a margin of freedom even in the fixity of destinies.

144

*

* *

Therefore, contrary to what the omnipotentialist zealots — those who wish to explain everything by the Divine Power — seem to understand, the Omnipotence of God does not coincide with the supreme All-Possibility. Omnipotence — already relative because situated at the degree of Being and thereby included in *Māyā* — possesses all power over the manifestations of this supreme Possibility; but the latter, by the very fact that it pertains to the Absolute, escapes the ontological jurisdiction of said power: God has all power over a given evil, but not over evil as such.[11] He may not create a given world, but He cannot not create the world as such; He cannot arrange that the Absolute not be absolute, that the Infinite not be infinite, that the world not be the world; that God not be God. If "I will be gracious to whom I will be gracious and will shew Mercy on whom I will shew Mercy" *(Exodus,* XXXIII, 19), it is because things and creatures are what they are in accordance with their possibility. God's attitude towards a creature is ultimately an aspect of the creature.

From the point of view of total Truth, there is an interdependence between the human person and the personal God, which can be explained by the fact that both are encompassed by *Māyā;* the exoterists are logically wrong — but could they do otherwise? — to lend to the Divinity-*Māyā* the characteristics of pure *Ātmā,* of the pure Absolute. The result of all this is the image of a God both anthropomorphic and incomprehensible, because inevitably

11. We have no doubt made this observation more than once and we shall perhaps return to it again, but it is scarcely possible, given the difficulty of the subject matter and given the quantity of doctrinal data, to remember all that has been expressed already from the point of view both of content and form; all the more so in that it is difficult to resist the intellectual temptation to define accurately that which demands a maximum of clarity.

145

contradictory; an image that is coupled with that of a man considered incapable of other than sensory knowledge, and held within the limits of a pious unintelligence by fundamentally moralistic arguments.

Moreover, the legitimate need for logical causal explanations of the disciplined and intuitive man is one thing, and the insatiable curiosity of the worldly and skeptical man is another; it is the latter that one refuses to answer by referring instead to the grandeur of God and the littleness of man; all the more so in that the exteriorized and exteriorizing spirit can never be satisfied, and even has no interest in being satisfied. Be that as it may, the Bible and the Koran demonstrate that the ancient Near Easterners, besides their quality of being "all of one piece," incontestably had about them something earthbound, inconstant and rebellious — they were surely not alone in having these weaknesses — which adds a justification to the onnipotentialist arguments on the part of the Scriptures.

*

* *

According to the logic of the obedientialist zealots, man is "slave" *('abd)* in the same unconditional manner that God is "Lord" *(Rabb)*. According to this way of looking at things, man has his intelligence only for taking note, through the study of the Revelation, of what God has declared to be good or bad; not for comprehending what is good or bad in itself and which God, in conformity with His Nature, has declared to be such. Through excess of piety — a piety that lends an absolute character to something necessarily relative and conditional, namely obedience — one does not even feel that it is absurd to tell us that God is just or compassionate, while proclaiming in the same breath that it is God who decides — as a tyrant would — what justice and compassion are.

A consequence of this so to speak "slavist" anthropology is the exaggeration, not of hell, but of the risk of falling into it; a risk attributed even to the most pious men and notwithstanding an equally intense correlative accentuation of the motive of hope, of pardon, of divine Clemency. No doubt, the perspective of Mercy reestablishes the balance in the eschatological doctrine as a whole, but it does not thereby abolish the excesses of the opposite perspective, nor the incompatibility between the two theses; for if it is true, according to Ghazali, that God has created sinners in order to be able to pardon them, and that, according to the caliph Ali, to despair of Mercy is a sin greater than all other sins combined, it cannot also be true that saintly men like Abu Bakr and Omar had reason — supposing the information is exact — to regret their human birth on account of the rigor of Judgement. One and the same doctrine cannot cite the example of a saint who would feel happy to spend only a thousand years in hell, and at the same time assure us that God pardons the repentant believer even if the mass of his sins reaches as far as heaven; and one and the same morality cannot in good logic bludgeon us with eschatological threats, objectively causing despair, while enjoining us to enjoy given "licit" pleasures of life, and not the least of them.

As for attributing to the human being an exclusively "obedient" nature — to an extent that practically amounts to taking away his prerogative as man — we would say first of all that man must obey when he has to accept a destiny, or a dogma that is incomprehensible a priori — but always guaranteed by other comprehensible and fundamental dogmas — or when he has to submit to a law or a rule; but he does not obey when he distinguishes one thing from another or when he notes that two and two make four. In any case, the decisive argument in this matter is the following: the fact that man can conceive Beyond-Being proves that he cannot be in every respect a "servant" *('abd)*, and that there is something in him — either in principle only or also in fact — that permits him to not reduce his spiritual activity to obedience pure and sim-

147

ple. This is what is expressed by the title of "vicar" *(khalīfah)* given to man by the Koran, and this is what is also expressed by the fact, again according to the Koran, that God breathed into man "of His Spirit" *(min Rūḥihi)*, thus granting him a real participation in the divine Spirit; something which, like the general phenomenon of human deiformity, excludes a nature capable only of submission, hence of servitude alone.[12] In other words, the human spirit is essentially endowed with objectivity. Man is capable — whether the relativists like it or not — of stepping outside his subjectivity, and this relates to his capacity of conceiving Beyond-Being, thus of transcending the domain of creating, revealing and legislating Being: of intellectually and contemplatively transcending the divine "I," the self-determination of the supreme Self.

This last remark permits us to mention the following aspect of the problem: the immanent Self comprises both Being and Beyond-Being. Now, to transcend the regimen of Being by virtue of a concrete and sufficient consciousness of Beyond-Being — a consciousness that is extremely rare and by definition unitive to some degree — is to transcend the Law, product of legislating Being; not by disdaining it *de facto,* but by perceiving its formal limits.[13] It is appropriate here to stress, in spite of its evidentness, that the immanent Self is transcendent in relation to the "I,"

---

12. Another example of what could justly and without misuse of language be termed "human dignity," is the title "friend of God" *(khalīl Allāh)* conferred by Islam upon Abraham. And when Jesus speaks of "our Father who art in Heaven," it is precisely in order to indicate that, if man is "servant" in a certain respect, he is "child" or "heir" in another.

13. The interiorization of the Law by Christ, and then by Saint Paul, pertains to this mystery; interiorization of the "letter which killeth," brought about by virtue of the "spirit which giveth life." Let it be noted that in Christ's intention this transfer of the form to the essence is not an "abolition" but a "fulfillment." That Christianity, being a religion, became "Law" in its turn, pertains to a completely different dimension.

otherwise the ego would be divine, whereas the transcendent Principle — conceived objectively — is immanent in all that exists, otherwise there would be no existence. And just as the Self does not cease to be immanent and virtually accessible on account of its transcendence, so too does the objective Principle not cease to be transcendent on account of its ontological immanence within creation.

*
* *

What partisans of an absolute determinism do not realize is that by abolishing secondary causes to the advantage of one single Cause — by recognizing only the latter to the detriment of the former — they compromise the notion of the divine Freedom, for a world with no liberty whatever, hence without the causality proper to it, cannot be derived from a free Divinity. The causative power of beings and things testifies to the one Power, it does not abolish it; man's liberty testifies to the liberty of God, in the sense that man is responsible for his acts because God is sovereignly free. The universe is not a clockwork, it is a living mystery; to affirm the contrary amounts to denying the Immanence which is ultimately an effect of Transcendence. And it is contradictory, to say the least, to maintain vehemently the absolute duality "Lord and servant" while declaring that only the Lord is.

But there is more: a God who demands obedience must Himself obey something, if it be permissible to express oneself thus; the God who obeys is the "non-supreme" *(apara)* of the Vedantists, who is already comprised within *Māyā*. A God who has nothing to obey does not demand obedience; and this is the "Supreme Divinity" *(Paramātmā)*, the "unqualified" *(nirguna)* Essence. God can obey only His own Nature; it is out of the question that He obey something supposedly situated outside Himself.

Or again: God-Essence is beyond good and evil, and is not an interlocutor; God-Person is an interlocutor, and loves good and demands that we love it. A God who, being the "Sovereign Good," loves and orders good, could not be "above good and evil," any more than a God possessing this indifference could order or forbid anything whatsoever.[14]

Instead of saying: "It is impossible for God, who is the Sovereign Good and who forbids evil, to will, create and do evil," the omnipotentialists prefer to say: "It is impossible for things to exist which God, who is the All-Powerful, has not willed and has not created, even evil things." On the one hand, the divine Essence, which is impersonal, is "personalized," and on the other hand, the personal God is "dehumanized."

*

* *

The great enigma — from the human point of view — is the question of knowing, not why evil as such is possible, but what the meaning is of the possibility of a given evil; evil can be understood abstractly, but not concretely — except for certain categories whose logic is transparent[15] — whereas good in all its forms can be understood concretely, that is, its possibility or necessity can be grasped without any difficulty. The fact is that in evil there is all the mystery of the absurd, and the absurd coincides with the unintelligible. Our only resource in that case is to refer to the notion of All-Possibility, but then we are once again within the abstract, phenomenologically speaking, although not in respect of intellection and con-

14. This amoral — not immoral — indifference appears in the Hindu notion of *Līlā*, the "divine Play" in and by *Māyā*.

15. It should not be forgotten that certain evils, natural catastrophes for example, are not evils in themselves, since the elements which provoke them are goods; it is true that the damage wrought by them on the human plane does not manifest anything positive, yet they are not intrinsically evil.

templation. All-Possibility is one thing, its contents are another.

Let us specify once again, even though this follows on the whole from what we have just said, that evil becomes incomprehensible to the extent that it is particular: the possibility of ugliness is graspable, but the "why" of a given particular ugliness, whether physical or moral, is not evident. What nonetheless in a certain sense explains a specific flaw — that is, the possibility, and in fact the necessity, of a particular, concrete and not merely principial defect — is the limitlessness of the Possible, which must realize abnormal possibilities that serve to belie impossibilities: what Possibility cannot realize in things as such — on pain of ontological absurdity — it realizes at least in appearances; on this plane, nothing is "impossible," even down to the most insignificant "substitutes" for impossibility.

A key to the enigma of evil in general is the following cosmogonic fatality: where there is form, there is not only difference, but also possibility of effective opposition, in accordance with the very level of formal coagulation. It has been said that the fall of Adam entailed that of all earthly creatures; consequently it actualized latent oppositions and introduced into the world struggle and hatred, hence evil as privation of charity; combined at times with an excess of rightness, as in the case of a just vengeance which exceeds its bounds.

*
* *

A typical example of obedientialist theology is the Asharite theory which in substance denies that God commands what is good and forbids what is evil; it asserts on the contrary — and we have already alluded to it above — that good is what God commands, and evil what He forbids. Now if such were the case, God would have no reason for commanding or forbidding anything whatever, for one does not command in order to command or forbid

151

in order to forbid, anymore than one permits in order to permit. Ashari's idea is that God "creates" both good and evil, an idea that is insufficient to say the least, since the cause of good, and thereby the distinction between good and evil, does not lie in the arbitrary act of a divine Subject already tainted with Relativity or with *Māyā,* but lies in the very Nature of God or in His Essence. It is in this sense that the Koran declares that God "hath prescribed Mercy for Himself," or "it is incumbent upon Him to aid the believers"; the Koran does not say that God "created" Mercy together with its contrary or its absence, without anyone being able to understand the content of these "creations," or without anyone being able to understand anything other than the fact of the divine decision. It could be argued that all this is ascribable to theological strategy: and in fact, in the mind of the theologian, it is a question of stressing that "God" — the Divine Subject who "wills" this or that — determines everything and is determined by nothing. However, it would have been enough to say that God commands or blesses what is in conformity with His Nature which is the Sovereign Good, which we are able to grasp through its reflections in creation. Two and two make four, not because God "wills" it, but because it results from His Essence;[16] and that is why He "wills" it in regard to men, in the sense that He renders it evident to them by providing them with intelligence. God wills us to participate in His Nature because He is the Sovereign Good and for no other reason.

One could point out in this connection that God, although "bound" by His own Nature to the verity that given causes engender given effects, is nevertheless free to choose the mode of operation on the one hand, and its terms on the other; the choice stems from His Infinitude,

---

16. This is why the word *Ḥaqq,* meaning both "Truth" and "Reality," is one of the Names of God.

whereas the coherence within the application of that choice stems from His Absoluteness. We would also stress again that liberty lies in the choice and not in the consequences of that choice, and that the right use of freedom therefore presupposes the knowledge of what our option implies; this is true even for God, notwithstanding the fact that His Omnipotence — His Freedom precisely — implies the capacity to bring about miraculous exceptions which nonetheless "prove the rule." Man, on the contrary, cannot under any circumstances choose a crystal and then choose that it be neither hard nor transparent. Be that as it may, it is not a matter of denying that consequences or modalities stem from the divine Will, but simply of emphasizing that they stem from it in a different way than causes or substances: in a certain manner, each drop of rain is linked to the divine Will by the fact that it is a possibility; but none is linked thereto in the same sense as is water as such, since it is by its very nature that water determines all its possible modes, and this nature is obviously willed by God.

*

* *

What the zealots of an ill-understood "divine Right" do not seem to understand is that in creating man, God binds Himself; thus He is no longer as absolutely free as He is in Himself. It is an error to say that He is unconditionally free with regard to man because He is unconditionally free in His own Nature; or to say that, having created man in accordance with a certain intention and hence in accordance with a certain logic, He did not commit Himself. A great theologian wrote that man owes everything to God but that God owes nothing to man, which amounts to saying that there is no logical relationship between the Creator and the creature; that in creating water for example, He could have created something which at any moment could cease to be water; or that God does not act justly be-

153

cause He is just, but that an act is just because it is accomplished by God.

The overaccentuation of Transcendence leads to the same impasse as the overaccentuation of Freedom or Omnipotence: for if there were only exclusive, hence absolutely separative Transcendence, there would be no way of knowing that God is transcendent, or even simply that He is. And likewise: if God were free or all-powerful in every respect possible — and He is so only in respect of the modes of His creation — He would be free to not have the Qualities which characterize Him, and even to not be God; *quod absit*. But for the thinker of the Asharite type, man has no choice: since he cannot know the absolutely Transcendent, he must limit himself to believing and submitting; now we would indeed like to know why. Quite fortunately, the religious feeling innate to man does not depend upon the pious excesses of a given theology, even if it accepts them on the plane of mental abstractions, through simple piety precisely.

If there is a world that exists before God and if moreover this world is differentiated, hence multiple, there must be in God Himself a principle of projection and differentiation and thereby of relativity, which affirms the hypostatic degrees within the Divine Order or simply the degrees of reality; in short, there must be a "metaphysical precedent" *in divinis* which renders both the world and things possible. When, out of concern for ontological unitarianism, this universal *Māyā* is denied, one ends up with the absurdity of a divine subjectivity both pitilessly transcendent and paradoxically anthropomorphic; therefore with the absurdity of a God who, through unitarianism, is obliged to take charge of everything; who in the absence of natural laws must create the burning of a fire each time there is one; of a God who "creates" the sins of men and who at the same time punishes them, except when He decides not to do so. All this we are supposed to accept for the simple reason that "God has so informed us," which

for the fideists takes the place of a metaphysical explanation, despite the fact that God created our intelligence and
with it our legitimate need for logical causal explanations.
The reason for man's creation is precisely the prodigy of
an intelligence capable of participating in the Nature of
God and its mysteries, and which, to the extent that it really participates in them, is the first to know that "the beginning of wisdom is the fear of God."

*

* *

In fact, there is not only a rational but also a moral logic;
and the latter, in its expressions, can violate the former.
The idea of an eternal hell, for example, is metaphysically
absurd; if it has been efficacious for more than two millen-
nia, that is because it has always been viewed according to
moral logic; this eternity then becomes the shadow of the
Divine Majesty that has been scorned. Whether it be a
question of damnation or of salvation, the absurdity lies in
the idea of an immortal soul beginning at birth and then
spending its eternity remembering its earthly situation,
and so on. The absurdity does not lie in a morally plausible symbolism, efficacious because it is founded on the
one hand upon what is quasi-absolute in the human condition, and on the other upon what, from the point of view
of this condition, is definitive as regards the destinies beyond the grave.

We could also express it thus: what religion wants to ob-
tain "at all costs," so to speak and thus to the possible detriment of logic, is for man to submit in every circumstance
to what is termed the "will of God," whether this be the Divine Mystery insofar as it may be incomprehensible to us,
or a given destiny that is difficult for us, or the unintelligible aspects of the world generally. And this gives to religious language or to theological formulation a certain
right to excessiveness, or even to the absurd, man being

155

what he is.[17] If there is a plane whereon "the end justifies the means," it is that of the spiritual life at every degree. "Blessed are those who have not seen and who have believed."

Let us here recall once again the difference between the "man of faith" and the "man of gnosis": it is the difference between the believer, who in all things has in view moral and mystical efficacy to the point of sometimes needlessly violating the laws of thought, and the gnostic, who lives above all from principial certitudes and who is so made that these certitudes determine his behavior and contribute powerfully to his alchemical transformation. Now, whatever be our vocational predispositions, we must needs realize a certain equilibrium between the two attitudes, for there is no perfect piety without knowledge, and there is no perfect knowledge without piety.

No doubt, there are men who save themselves limpingly, and there is certainly no reason to reproach them for it or to prevent them from doing so; but this does not mean that they alone are saved and that everyone else has to limp in order to be saved. This remark is valid independently of the fact that, in some respects, we all falter, if only on account of the uncertainties of our earthly condition.

*

* *

We have had recourse more than once to the Buddhist notion of *upāya*, the "saving stratagem": now an *upāya*, by the very fact that it is a means "sanctified by the end," has a certain right to sacrifice the truth to opportunity; that is, it has this right to the extent that a given truth remains foreign to its own fundamental truth and to the corresponding spiritual strategy.

17. This reminds us of the Zen *koans;* of formulas both meaningless and explosive, and intended to shatter the shell of mental habits that obstructs the vision of the Real.

An *upāya*, in order to be effective, must exclude; the way of "God as such" must exclude the way of "God become man" and conversely; but either way will retain a reflection of the other, the function of which will remain secondary. Islam, on pain of being ineffectual or something other than itself, must exclude the Christian dogma; Christianity for its part must exclude the characteristic axiom of Islam — as it excluded at the outset the axiom of Judaism, which in this connection coincides with that of Islam. The Epistles of Saint Paul show how the Apostle simplifies Mosaism with the intention of buttressing Christianity from the point of view of both doctrine and method; in an analogous manner, all that shocks Christians in Moslem imagery must be interpreted as a symbolism meant to clear the ground in view of the efficacy of the Muhammadan *upāya*. In order to understand a religion, it is useless to stop short at its extrinsic polemic; its fundamental intention lies in its intrinsic affirmation which testifies to God and leads to God. The imagery is nothing, the underlying geometry is everything.

Enigma and Message of Islamic Esoterism

Islamic esoterism presents an engima since, at first sight, it could reasonably be asked what is its origin — and even its specific nature. Indeed, if it be admitted on the one hand that Sufism is esoterism, and on the other that it appeared at the very beginning of Islam, then one becomes perplexed before the following phenomenon: Islam is a legalistic religion which takes no account of asceticism, whereas Sufism, on the contrary, is expressly ascetical. Thus the following question arises: what is the logical, organic and historical relationship between two traditions apparently so divergent, although of the same origin? It is not surprising that most Western Islamicists have assumed[1] that Sufism is of Christian or Hindu origin; the opinion is totally false, but benefits from extenuating circumstances, namely that the theoretical or practical eccentricities of Sufi asceticisms are all but incompatible with the message of sober equilibrium of Moslem legalism.

Although asceticism, by its very nature, by no means coincides with esoterism, it must be said, in the case of Islam and taking into account profound intentions, that the incompatibility between religious legalism and Sufi asceticism is none other, after all, than the incompatibility that has everywhere and always opposed the common religion

---

1. Before Massignon and Nicholson at least.

and the initiatory dimension. It is true that this incompatibility — due to the difference of levels and ends — goes hand in hand with a compensatory compatibility based on the identity between a traditional symbolism and psychological and moral tendencies, but this incompatibility is nonetheless inevitable since between form and essence there is not only analogy and continuity, but also opposition and discontinuity.[2] From the point of view of the Moslem religion, asceticism is meaningless unless it is in a legal form that wisely canalizes and delimits it, either by means of various prohibitions — above all alimentary and sexual[3] — or through the annual fast of Ramadan. From the point of view of Sufism, on the contrary, either exterior practices are secondary — this is the interiorizing perspective of gnosis, that only seldom asserts itself — or else they are elements of ascesis which it is good to multiply and amplify, or even exaggerate, as does ordinary Sufism. Parallel to asceticism there is the deepening of the virtues which asceticism is supposed to bring about but which in reality does not necessarily depend upon it; according to its levels, this deepening can either refine the moral qualities, or open the heart to immanent illuminations.

Not only the historical testimonies but also the simple nature of things — outlined above with regard to the subject matter under consideration — oblige us to acknowledge that the Prophet instituted two relatively different

2. The proof that this aspect of opposition was manifested from the outset, is furnished by this disclosure of Abu Hurayrah: "I have guarded in my memory two precious treasures of knowledge which I have received from the Messenger of God. One of them I have made public; but if I were to divulge the other, you would cut my throat." An analogous saying is found in the Gospel of Saint Thomas. *Spiritus ubi vult spirat* (*John*, III, 8).

3. There is also the prohibition — more or less relative — of music, poetry and dance; esoterism takes no notice of this, given that it refers to the nature of things, hence to intrinsic, and not legal or conventional, values.

traditional currents, at once solidary and divergent: the one legal, common and obligatory, and the other ascetical, particular and vocational. A question which thus arises is — although we have already touched upon the answer — if the most ancient testimonies of what later was called "Sufism" *(taṣawwuf)* point to an asceticism and nothing else, and if, in fact, Islamic esoterism recognizes itself in this asceticism, what is the relationship between the latter and the realities of esoterism? The answer is simple once account is taken of the fact that all esoterism comprises a purgative way: if the qualities of the "servant" — the contingent and imperfect subject — must be "extinguished" or must "disappear" *(fanā)* in order to allow the Qualities of the Lord — the absolute and perfect Subject — to penetrate, the human individual obviously must submit to disciplines which favor, if not actually effectuate, this initiatory and alchemical process. But this way of looking at things precludes the perspective of merit reinforced by a voluntarist and sentimental individualism which so frequently appears in what we have termed "average Sufism," and in fact reduces a purgative alchemy to a penitential mysticism.

*

* *

Esoterism comprises three unequal dimensions which combine to a varying extent, according to level and temperament: first of all, the ascetical dimension, which Sufism claims, precisely, and in which it seems to recognize itself; secondly, the invocatory dimension, encompassing all that Sufism means by *Dhikr,* "Remembrance (of God)"; and thirdly, the intellective dimension, which comprises the metaphysical truths and requires discernment, meditation and contemplation. Now the abusive emphasis upon the first dimension causes the weakening of the third, and conversely; but not symmetrically, for when the intellective dimension is emphasized, the ascetical dimen-

161

sion is not thereby deprived of its qualities, but merely made superfluous, to a certain degree, by the concrete results of gnosis. In the same way, the perspective of "fear," *makhāfah*, necessarily becomes more transparent and more serene through the effects of the perspective of "knowledge," *ma'rifah.*[4]

The intermediary dimension, which we could qualify as "sacramental" on account of the use it makes of sacred Formulas and Divine Names, is so to speak neutral: in it the two other dimensions — the first "peripheral" and the third "central" — meet and combine. The third dimension transcends the outer religion on the one hand by the doctrine, founded upon the ideas of "absolute Unity" *(Wahdaniyah)* or of "Essence" *(Dhāt)* — of "Beyond-Being" if one will, in the sense of *Paramātmā* — then of "Veil" *(Hijāb)* in the sense of *Māyā*, and finally, of "Union" *(Ittihād)* in the sense of *Moksha;* on the other hand, this dimension of gnosis goes beyond the common religion by its particular end in view — expressed precisely by the term *Ittihād* — which transcends the quest of elementary salvation. From this stem certain paradoxical expressions such as the disdain for Paradise, which is not to be taken literally, however — for supreme Union does not exclude in every respect the Paradise of the houris, any more than the divine nature of the *Avatāra* excludes the human nature.

It will rightly be said that asceticism and morality do not in themselves constitute esoterism, and one will not be mistaken in rejecting a priori the equation "ascesis equals esoterism," made by a number of Sufis; but one must accept the fact that in Islam asceticism pertains, technically and traditionally, to esoterism alone, and that in consequence the above equation possesses a *de facto* justification which it is impossible not to take into account.

---

4. "It is not I who have left the world, it is the world that has left me"; a key saying which we have quoted more than once.

Enigma and Message of Islamic Esoterism

*

* *

The apparently problematical — but in reality elliptical — equation "esoterism equals ascesis" means in substance: esoterism is the elimination of the individual obstacles which prevent or "veil" the irradiation of the divine
Self in the soul. Concrete formulations of this equation
are, for example, the following: "Sufism (taṣawwuf) is
fasting"; "Sufism is silence"; "Sufism is solitude"; "Sufism
is poverty"; and other expressions of the kind. Each of
these negative conceptions has the implicit meaning of the
removal of an obstacle in view of the "unveiling" of the
one Reality.[5]

This insistence of a certain esoterism upon the ascetical
dimension which is after all merely secondary and conditional, could not be explained if this esoterism did not address itself to a large collectivity rather than to a restricted
elite only; for in the latter case, esoterism would be defined by its essence, namely an integral metaphysical doctrine, and such a doctrine is spiritually operative only for
the "pneumatics," not for the "psychics"; thus for a minor-
ity, not for the majority. The idea of an esoterism addressing itself to all from the outset, will seem quite paradoxical
and even heterodox to those who have a too systematic
and in fact unrealistic idea of esoterism, yet it testifies to a
possibility that lies in the nature of things, which is to say
that vulgarized esoterism draws its justification from a certain efficaciousness. Moreover, we do not even have the
choice: we are obliged to note the historical phenomenon
such as it is, and to accept the existence of an esoterism
that precisely addresses itself in principle to a large num-

5. No doubt there are also positive definitions, such as this one from
Ghazali: "Sufism is a taste (dhawq)"; in this case, the ellipsis refers to
subjective experience, not to objective nature, it has thus an indirect
character like the ascetical allusions (ishārāt) just mentioned.

163

ber if not literally to all. Certainly, this "expanded" esoterism always contains authentic wisdom in some sector; it has its secrets, but only in its "kernel" *(lubb)*, not in its "shell" *(qishr);* it is not itself wisdom, but thanks to its system of degrees of inwardness the specific nature of pure esoterism is preserved, wherever it can and must assert itself.

As is proved on the one hand by history, and on the other by the great diffusion of the initiatory orders, there is an esoterism that is preached; only integral gnosis is not preached. Primitive Christianity, being at first an esoterism by virtue of its perspective of "inwardness" — to the detriment of outwardness, hence its heterodoxy from the point of view of the Law of Moses — spread through preaching. The same is true for Sufism, which is esoteric by virtue of its perspective of "spiritual path," hence of "realization," and "transmutation," a perspective foreign to the exoteric Law. Sufism, like Christianity, possesses its mysteries and thereby its secrets; nonetheless, in both cases there is a message addressed "to many," if not "to all."

Thus, whether one likes it or not, initiatory propaganda exists and indeed has existed from the beginning;[6] what does not exist, and has never existed, is propaganda for doctrines that are necessarily secret and for their corresponding particular means; and even in this case the necessity for secrecy or discretion is only extrinsic and varies in accordance with the human milieu and cyclic conditions. The absence of an intermediate term between the outer and the inner faces of the tradition is not conceiva-

---

6. During the 19th century, the Shaykh Al-Baddi succeeded in affiliating the entire Berber tribe of the Ida Ou-Ali to the *Tarīqah Tijāniyah;* this is far from initiatory elitism, whose principle however is not rejected wherever necessity demands it. And it is known that the spread of Islam in India is due, not to force of arms, but to conversion due in large part to the propaganda of the Brotherhoods.

ble even theoretically, for such an abrupt confrontation would not be viable; similarly, the confrontation between the world and God is inconceivable without the presence of a celestial and quasi-divine world on the one hand, and a hypostatic prefiguration of the world in God on the other. It is thus that in ordinary Sufism a refined or intensified exoterism is combined with a vulgarized and moral esoterism, and we observe analogous symbioses in India and elsewhere; even *Advaita-Vedānta* has its popular prolongations in Shivite surroundings.

Mysticism results from the tendency towards inwardness, towards inner experience; it is "supernaturally natural" to man, which is to say that it corresponds to an innate need and is found wherever there is a religion, legalism being unable to satisfy all aspirations. Thus, mysticism cannot not be; the knowledge of its levels, its degrees, its lines of demarcation is another matter altogether.[7]

*

* *

More than once we have had occasion to notice the intrusion of fideist attitudes into the domain of Sufism; our present context allows us to give yet another example of it, attributed rightly or wrongly to Ibn Arabi.[8] In several passages the Koran says that "God sat upon the Throne";

---

7. Despite their fundamental identity, there is a certain gap between primitive Sufism which was an ascetical and empiricist mysticism, and the doctrinal Sufism of the Middle Ages, which used a largely Hellenistic terminology. Ibn Arabi was the first to formulate the doctrine of "ontological monism" *(waḥdat al-Wujūd* = "unicity of the Real")*, which may explain, aside from other perhaps less plausible or in any case controversial reasons, the honorific title of *Shaykh al-akbar* conferred upon him by some.

8. Cf. *La Profession de Foi*, translation by R. Deladrière. Someone has brought to our attention that this treatise is not by Ibn Arabi but by one of his disciples, which we readily believe, but the question is without importance here.

now, like the Hanbalites, the Sufi author believes that one should not try to interpret, thus to understand, this image, and he blames people for wanting to see in the "Session of God" *(istiwā')* a symbolism of "elevation," "domination" or "superiority"; he even concludes that all this is "merely presumption," given that the "Ancients" never transmitted any commentary. We think on the contrary that this omission cannot be legally binding, for the simple reason that it is not the role of the Ancients to explain everything, above all when evident things are concerned. Now it is evident that the Divine Throne cannot but signify, a priori, that which a throne as such signifies, namely, authority and royalty, hence superiority, power, justice, and on the whole, majesty; if words have a meaning, which precisely our fideists seem to contest. They would like to make us admit that faith could require the acceptance of an image that has no meaning and whose reason for being we are forbidden to seek; or in other words, that God could propose an image merely in order to propose it, an image therefore which means nothing, and that He could moreover make of it a condition *sine qua non* of faith. In reality, if God spoke of a "session" and not of another act, and of a "throne" and not of another object, it is obviously because He wished to point out something definite and comprehensible: to seat oneself upon a throne is to assume a function of authority with regard to a given individual or collectivity. Obviously God possesses authority in an by his intrinsic Nature; He thus possesses it in an immutable manner, but actualizes it only starting from the cosmogonic "moment" when the singular or collective correlative comes into existence; this is what is meant by the "Divine Session."

In any case, to maintain that the only legitimate commentary *(ta'wīl)* of a sacred expression is the registering of the word, is a contradiction in terms; it is as much as to say that the translation of a foreign word lies in the mere phenomenon of the sound.

*

* *

Islam as such offers the believer ideas and means enabling him to reach Paradise, on condition that they be accepted and put into practice with sincerity. Sufism for its part presents the nothingness of our contingency in relation to the Absolute with a moral coloration which in fact — whether we like it or not — leads us to the Augustinian and Lutheran conception of the irremediable corruption of human nature. Assuredly, the awareness of the incommensurability between the contingent and the Absolute is a preparation for the initiatory realization of the Self, starting from the ego; but its individualistic, voluntaristic and sentimental presentation has nothing to do with gnosis, and introduces into Islam a mystical moralism which on the whole is foreign to the sober realism of this religion, and which explains to a great extent the hostility of the ulamas, and also of the philosophers, who at times are closer to wisdom than to simple rationality. Be that as it may, when saints regret not having been born as birds or as blades of grass, or when they would deem themselves happy to have to spend only a thousand years in the fires of Hell, and other extravagances of the kind, it is always possible to think that they refer, basically, to the awareness of the incommensurability just mentioned, which is the first condition of unitive alchemy; but such symbolisms are nonetheless problematical by reason of their literal extravagance.

But here too there is a compensation: if the metaphysical gap between the "created" and the "Uncreated," or between the contingent and the Absolute, has been expressed in terms of moral individualism, the anthropological pessimism resulting from it has been able to serve in fact as the springboard for a mysticism of Mercy and hope — or for the "faith which saves." This is so in Islam as well as in Christianity and, farther away from us, in de-

167

votional and invocatory Buddhism founded upon the
Grace of Amitabha. For Mercy — or the divine Attraction — is actualized only in function of the awareness we
have of our nothingness, whether this awareness be metaphysical or moral, or both at once.[9]

*

* *

All these data allow one to consider a particular interpretation of the ternary *Sharī'ah-Ṭarīqah-Ḥaqīqah,* "Law-
Way-Truth": according to the common usage of the
terms, *Ṭarīqah* is the Way and *Ḥaqīqah* the Reality to be attained — at least when this last term is understood in connection with the one preceding it. But by *Ṭarīqah* we may
also understand the vast domain of ordinary Sufism, and
by *Ḥaqīqah* the restricted domain of quintessential Sufism,
hence of esoterism properly so called; the first is founded
upon anthropological pessimism, asceticism, the accumulation of meritorious practices and a scrupulous moralism,
and the second upon gnosis, both from the doctrinal and
operative points of view.

But let us return to the proper meaning of the word
Ṭarīqah: the "Way" essentially comprises "Stations,"
Maqāmāt; each fundamental virtue — that is, virtue unshakable when confronted by trials of discipline and destiny — is a necessary stage in the itinerary towards Union
or "Reality," *Ḥaqīqah.*[10] The ascetical character of primi-

9. It goes without saying that an awareness of our metaphysical
nothingness — although this unilateral awareness does not summarize
our entire nature — is necessarily accompanied by a corresponding
moral consciousness, which fact does not excuse the moral exaggerations of some; for the quantitative character of these excesses of zeal is,
precisely, opposed to the metaphysical quality of the awareness in
question.
10. The *Ṭarīqah* coincides with the "straight (ascending) Path" *(Sirāṭ
mustaqīm)* of the canonical prayer; this "straight Path" — in the words

tive Sufism and of the average Sufism of the following centuries, is explained positively by this theory of "Stations," that progressively lift the "veils" before "Reality." In defining Sufism as an ascesis, it is implicitly defined as a succession of realizatory and liberating Stations; and this corresponds perfectly to the specific nature of esoterism, which "transforms" man instead of simply saving him; or rather, which saves him in transforming him, and transforms him in saving him.

The initiatory pact, in Islam, relates to holy war; the initiates are the "combatants" *(mujāhidūn);* the initiatory path being, according to the Prophet himself, the "great holy war" *(al-jihād al-akbar)*. Now all the modes of asceticism — fasting, vigils, solitude, silence, accumulation of meritorious acts — are so many ways of combating the "soul which incites to evil" *(an-nafs al-ammārah)*, and this explains positively the association of ideas between esoterism and ascesis, or rather the equation that seemingly reduces the first element to the second, but which also has the meaning of a veiling of that which is uncovered only at the cost of a trial and thanks to an illuminative opening. As Al-Hallaj said: "Let no one drink the wine if he is not a hero; if he has not abandoned sleep, and unless his eyelids no longer close." The enigma of Sufism is that the thing is designated by the price it is worth; that the celestial value is expressed in terms of earthly sacrifice.

*

* *

of this prayer (the *Fātihah)* — is the path "of those on whom Thou bestowest Thy Grace" *(an'amta 'alayhim)*, namely on the initiates *(mutabārikūn)*, according to the esoterically evident meaning; it is not the descending path "of those against whom Thou art angered" *(maghdūb 'alayhim)*, namely the unbelievers and the proud sinners, nor the horizontal and zigzaging path "of those who go astray" *(dāllūn)*, who are here the profane and lukewarm believers.

Islam draws all its strength from the evidence that the truth of the One, hence of the Absolute, is the decisive truth, therefore the most important of all; and that man is saved, essentially and initially, by the acceptance of this supreme Truth. This possibility of acceptance of the transcendent Reality and the saving virtue of this acceptance, constitute so to speak the nature and the vocation of man.

The esoteric perspective grasps at the outset that the supreme Truth implies and demands, by its very nature and primacy, that we accept it entirely, therefore with all that we are. Esoterism is to exoterism what the sphere is to the circle; in the geometry of Islam, Sufism is in principle the third dimension, without which Islam is incomplete and after which there is no other. If we refer to the classic ternary *Imān-Islām-Iḥsān* — Faith, Resignation, spiritual Virtue — the geometric point will symbolize the first of these three elements, and the circle the second; the third will deepen and transpose the two preceding elements and thus will realize their universality and their essence. Likewise for the ternary *Sharī'ah-Ṭarīqah-Ḥaqīqah*, of which we have spoken above: whereas the second element prolongs the first while anticipating the third,[11] the latter transcends their common level and effectuates the universal tridimensionality.

*

* *

11. In principle but not in fact, the *Ṭarīqah* pertains entirely to the esoteric dimension, the *Ḥaqīqah* being the end to be attained or the always present essence; the non-extension of the point — in our geometric symbolism — then marks formal fixation, whereas the roundness of both the circle and the sphere indicates the quality of the Essence and thereby of universality. According to another interpretation — sanctioned by the tradition — the circle is on the contrary the exterior domain, that of the *Sharī'ah;* the radii represent the diverse modes of the *Ṭarīqah;* the center is the *Ḥaqīqah.*

"I testify that there is no divinity but God alone, Who hath no associate": this Testification establishes the distinction, first of all between God and His counterfeits, then between God and the world, and finally between *Ātmā* and *Māyā*, or the Absolute and the relative; this third distinction pertains to integral metaphysics, and thereby to the esoteric perspective, since it even applies to the Divine Order, wherein it establishes a separation between the "relative Absolute" — namely Being — and the pure Absolute.

"I testify that Muhammad is His servant and messenger": this second Testification implicitly or symbolically describes the spiritual nature of man. The believer, in imitation of Muhammad, is "servant" in the sense that he must resign himself to the everywhere present Will of God, and he is "messenger" in the sense that he must participate in the divine Nature and, consequently, prolong it as it were, which precisely is possible by virtue of the prerogatives of human nature. Moslem fideism readily exaggerates the first of these qualities to the detriment of the most legitimate rationality; thus one must try to discover in its paradoxes, hyperboles and incoherences, the moral intentions and the implicit mystical meanings.[12] From the standpoint of this fideism, the simple nature of things is nothing, whereas the moral or ascetical intention is everything. The question remains to what extent the will can and must determine the intelligence in a voluntarist mystic, and to what extent, on the contrary, the intelligence can and must determine the will in the gnostic; the

---

12. One must exercise patience and charity, without lacking discernment. It should not be forgotten that the gift of discernment readily goes hand in hand with a certain impatience: with the underlying desire to compel the world to be logical, and with the difficulty of resigning oneself spontaneously to the metaphysical right of the world to a certain coefficient of absurdity.

latter relationship evidently has priority over the former, in principle if not always in fact.

Resignation to the divine Will at every moment, combined with the sense of the Absolute,[13] constitutes the entire powerful originality of the perspective, and thus the piety, of Islam; the Moslem is altogether "himself" wherever he feels united to the Will of God. "To extinguish oneself" or "to disappear" *(faniya)* in the Will of God, is at the same time, and correlatively, to be at the disposition of the Divine Presence *(Ḥuḍūr);* it is to allow free passage for the radiation of the Archetypes and the Essence; of that which pertains to "necessary Being" *(Wujūd muṭlaq),* and not merely to "possible being"; of That which cannot not be.

13. These two qualities, expressed by the second Testification, correspond to "Peace" *(Salām)* and to "Benediction" *(Ṣalāt)* in the Hommage to the Prophet *(Ṣalāt 'alā 'n-Nabī).* It could also be said that Benediction concerns the Intellect *(spiritus),* and Peace, the soul *(anima);* illumination and appeasement; certitude and serenity. And one knows the symbolism of the "purified" or "melted heart," and of the "expanded breast": the heart represents the Intellect both in respect of knowledge and of love, and the breast represents the soul freeing itself from "narrowness" and realizing itself by "expansion." Concerning the sense of the Absolute mentioned above, it is precisely the need for the Absolute which explains — and excuses, at least as regards the intention — the exaggerations that make the access to certain Moslem texts so difficult.

Pitfalls in the Language of Faith

In Christianity, as elsewhere, one finds typical examples in which, when speaking of human nature, the aspect "servant" is overemphasized. We say "overemphasized," not to imply that there are limits to the virtue of humility inasmuch as it is determined by an objectively real situation — lacking which there is excess and not norm — but to specify that a certain religious sentimentality is always quick to exaggerate man's unworthiness; that is, to reduce total and deiform man to partial and deviated man, and in some cases to reduce man as such to particular kinds of men. This in a sense is what happens when God is entreated, prior to the rite of Consecration, "to receive favorably this offering of your servants," or "to cause the Holy Spirit to descend" upon the Eucharistic elements and to change them "as a favor from Thy goodness" into the body and blood of Christ, and other formulas of the kind, according to the liturgies. Thus an objective and sacramental appearance is given to a subjective and moral disposition.

Saint Thomas, who is aware of the problem, asks first of all whether the supplication in question is not a "superfluous prayer since the divine Power infallibly produces the sacrament," and then answers on the one hand that "the efficacy of the sacramental words could be counteracted by the intention of the celebrant," and on the other hand that "it is not improper to ask God for what we are sure He will grant." Finally, he states that the priest prays, not in order that the sacrifice may be accomplished, but "that it be fruitful in us."[1] These explanations are plausible,[2] but they do not explain the reason for the formulations themselves, when that is the entire question from the point of view of religious language, which is what we are concerned with here, independently of liturgical variations.[3]

Another example of religious overemphasis is the following: The *Decree* of Gratian (12th century) stipulates that, if consecrated hosts remain after the Mass, the priests "must be careful to consume them with fear and trembling." It is true that the sense of the sacred excludes all casualness, but that is no reason for expressing oneself in such a manner as to give the impression of an irascible moralism rather than the vivifying and peace-giving hope which ought to be manifest here, and which the faithful ought to be capable of, on pain of being unqualified for the rite. What has priority in such a case is not an attitude of "trembling,"[4] but on the contrary, a contemplative rec-

---

1. Here Aquinas bases himself upon a text of Saint Augustine, which in its turn conveys an opinion of Paschasius Radbert; cf. *Summa Theologica*, Part Three, question 83.

2. Except perhaps in connection with the legitimacy of a request certain to be granted, for this legitimacy, if it is evident in some cases, does not seem evident to us in the case of a sacrament.

3. As regards the underlying intention — not the explicit form — of the eucharistic prayers, it has been asserted that these prayers can be explained by the unworthiness of man as such, and by the fact that the Mass is a "communal act," so that it is a matter of expressing the feeling of the congregation. Without wishing to dwell on this question which lies outside our subject, we shall point out that the conception of the more or less sacerdotal role of lay attendence˙is extremely ambiguous and can give rise to many abuses, in spite of theological boundaries which moreover differ from one confession to another.

4. An attitude which a Saint Julian Eymard, apostle of the worship of the Blessed Sacrament, would not have approved of. Let us add however that we greatly prefer the trembling of Gratian to the impertinence of the modernists.

ollection made of serenity and holy joy; a recollection by definition combined with reverential awe, to be sure, but not to the point of reducing the whole approach to a reflex of separation or withdrawal. The expression of Gratian serves basically to make one aware of the unconscious profanation involved when the eucharistic sacrament is vulgarized by a piety more emotive than realistic, and forgetful of the injunction not to give "unto the dogs what is holy";[5] forgetful also of the principle that charity rightly understood depends upon truth, hence upon the nature of things.

In this context, the golden chalice of the Mass comes to mind, and we remember another expression testifying to the occasional "ostracism" of religious sentimentality: more than once, we have read that gold is merely a "vile metal" whereas it is the soul that is beautiful, and other expressions of the kind. In reality, the fact that gold is matter in no way makes it "vile," otherwise the consecrated host and *a fortiori* the bodies of Christ and of the Virgin — raised up to Heaven and not destroyed — would also be "vile," *quod absit.* One has to be affected by a fundamentally moralizing mentality to confuse in practice a merely existential inferiority with moral lowness. The very fact that the chalice of the Mass must be golden belies such a misuse of terminology and the irreverent association of ideas it logically entails. We would not have mentioned such a misuse were it not for many other examples of the

---

5. There is, besides, something singularly disproportionate or "ill-sounding" in the fact of consuming the consecrated hosts for the mere reason that there are too many of them and that one does not wish to save them. There is a dissonance here which in its own way points to the disparity between the sacrament and a certain interpretation lacking in realism and suppleness; it is to underestimate God through excess of zeal.

175

kind in pious literature,[6] at least when the subject dealt with invites to such confusions; the fundamental "complex" always being the scorn of the "flesh" in the name of the "spirit," or of nature in the name of the supernatural, whether rightly or wrongly.

Since in the preceding chapters we have amply referred to Islamic theology, it is no doubt worth pointing out again certain pitfalls which make access to the pious literature of Islam singularly troublesome, and which in many cases may even block it. There is first of all a marked tendency towards elliptical expression, and also, almost correlatively, a no less disconcerting tendency towards hyperbolism or simply exaggeration.[7] This is not to say — as we have seen — that Christianity is free from this kind of pitfall, but its language is on the whole more "Aryan" than that of Moslem piety, hence more direct and more open, also less symbolist and less florid, so that it runs fewer risks as regards its subject matter. For the Westerner, exaggeration is something intellectually inadequate and morally dishonest; for the Near-Easterner, its falseness is compensated by its usefulness: it emphasizes the truth by stylizing it, releasing thereby the underlying intention of the image it amplifies; exaggeration almost takes on the function of "essentialization," so that it sometimes appears as "truer" than its object, thus revealing its secret quality, blurred by the veil of contingencies. The quantitative — not qualitative — character of exaggeration takes nothing away from its forcefulness in the eyes of those who accept and practice it, and we believe that this is not

6. In this order of ideas, one readily overlooks the dignity and innocence of animals, which have to bear the terminological brunt of the human fall.

7. We have dealt amply with this thorny question in the first three chapters of our book *Sufism: Veil and Quintessence.*

unconnected with the prestige of the idea of "power," hence also with the argument of Omnipotence.

Symbolism is the primordial language, that of the *Sophia Perennis;* the question is to know what its duties and its rights are; the answers will doubtless vary according to temperaments and epochs.

*

* *

Many paradoxes of Islamic literature, beginning with the *aḥādīth* themselves, can be explained by an ellipticalness whose intention is to cause a "catalyzing shock," without regard to even elementary logic. Common sense then appears as something "outward" and "superficial," profane if one will, hence as a lack of penetration, intuition and subtlety; the very paradox of the ellipses is supposed to stimulate our awareness of underlying intentions.

As an example we shall give the following *ḥadīth,* whose authenticity, by the way, cannot be guaranteed, which hardly matters, since Moslems quote it without hesitation: "The purest food is that which we earn by the work of our hands; the Prophet David worked with his own hands to earn his bread. The merchant who conducts his affairs honestly and without desire to cheat others, will be placed in the hereafter amongst the Prophets, the saints and the martyrs."

Against this discourse, of a flagrant absurdity if taken literally, one could immediately raise the objection that David was a king and that the question of manual work did not arise for him. Nonetheless, one could imagine that he intended to give a good example to his people and that he did not consider royalty as labor to be remunerated; this point is not very important, but since the image of a king who believes himself obliged to work to earn his food is absurd in itself, it is worth pointing out its possible plausibility. But let us pass to the essential: a merchant is a

177

Survey of Metaphysics and Esoterism

priori interested in earning as much as possible, and the temptation to small or large fraud lies in the trade itself;[8] to resist this temptation methodically, hence to renounce fundamentally the instinct for gain, on the basis of faith in God, thus on the basis of a spiritual ideal, is to die to a mode of subjectivity; objectivity, whether intellectual or moral, is in fact a kind of death.[9] Now objectivity, which after all is the essence of the human vocation, is a mode of sanctity, and it even coincides with sanctity to the extent that its content is elevated or that it is integral. The detachment of the merchant, for the love of God, is "one kind of sanctity," which, when one considers its substance, coincides with "sanctity as such"; whence, in the *hadīth* quoted above, the reference to the saints and even to the Prophets.[10] The saying is scandalous at first glance, but for that very reason it incites to meditation.

That dialectical and symbolist ellipticalness can give rise to many abuses, or that it can even make one lose the critical sense which it is supposed to stimulate, is quite obvious but it is not the issue. Be that as it may, "The gods love obscure language," as a Hindu text says; they love this language, not because they affect unintelligibility, but because they hate profanation; take away the vice of profanity from souls, and the gods will take away the veil of obscurity from their language. The question is to what extent man has a right to this principle; to what extent he can speak in the name of the gods, and like the gods.

8. Avidity is even considered, in the Koran, as the vice typifying fallen man: "Rivalry (for increasing gain) distracts ye (from God), until ye visit the tombs . . ." (Sura "Rivalry," 1 and 2).

9. In the East we have often met with the detachment and the serenity resulting from this attitude; and this in merchants who usually were poor, most of them members of a Brotherhood.

10. The words "amongst the Prophets" indicate, not celestial localization, but affinity with the attitude in question, namely that of detachment "for the sake of the Face of God" *(liwajhi 'Llāh)*.

178

*

* *

But there are not only elliptical expressions of a paradoxical appearance, there are also symbolical, analogical and allusive expressions. In this connection we shall quote the following utterances, attributed to the caliph Ali:[11] "If even a single drop of wine were to fall into a well, which afterwards one were to fill in order to build a minaret there, I would not climb that minaret to make the call to prayer. If one drop of wine were to fall into a river, which were then to dry up and grasses grow on its bed, I would not pasture an animal there." Taken literally, these utterances are properly absurd because contrary to the nature of things, both with respect to wine and to its prohibition. In reality, wine in itself is noble — as is proved by the wedding of Cana and the euchararistic rite — and the Koran forbids it only because of the danger of drunkenness, hence of irresponsibility, quarreling and murder, and for no other reason. Contrary to the nature of wine and to the intention of the Law, the quoted utterances logically amount to saying on the one hand that wine is intrinsically bad, and on the other that this is why the Law forbids it. Traditionally, it is said that in Paradise wine will be permitted; and no one is unaware that Christ, Moses, Abraham and Noah drank wine, in short that all the ancient Semites did, as Jews and Christians still do, and honorably so; it is also known that in Sufism the symbolism of wine plays a positive role.[12] The absurdity of the saying quoted

---

11. Rightly or wrongly; but that is not the question since they are related without hesitation. What counts here is the multitude and success of utterances of this type and not their authenticity.

12. Witness the *Khamriyah,* the celebrated mystical poem of Omar ibn Al-Farid. In his quatrains, Omar Khayyam expresses astonishment that wine is prohibited here below, while in Paradise it will be permitted; a sally which is meaningful only in esoterism.

179

is so flagrant that it is this very dissonance which permits one to suppose — or which obliges one to admit — that there is here an allusive and analogical intention.[13] Consequently, the issue is not wine in itself but the negative or malefic principle of psychic drunkenness; natural and individualistic, not supernatural and liberating, drunkenness. It is this aspect of inebriation that intervenes to some degree in profane music, or in music assimilated in a profane manner, amplifying the ego instead of enabling it to transcend itself.[14] The result is a narcissism refractory to spiritual discipline, an adoration of self that is at the antipodes of the beatific extinction of which sacred art intends to give a presentiment. When hearing beautiful music, the guilty will feel innocent; the contemplative, on the contrary, when hearing the same music, will forget himself by having a presentiment of the essences; metaphorically speaking, he will find his life in losing it, or he will lose it in finding it. That is, for the contemplative, music evokes all the mystery of the return of the accidents to the Substance.[15]

But let us return to the *ḥadīth* of Ali: in summary, the animosity of the fourth caliph towards wine is explained when one admits that practically wine amounts to pride; the narcissistic inflation produced by drunkenness is in

---

13. *Credo quia absurdum est,* as Tertullian said.

14. Except in the case where it constitutes a "sensible consolation," either peace-giving or stimulating, and without pretension; but the Islamic perspective excludes even this possibility, at least in principle.

15. Christianity is a musical religion, if one may say so, as is indicated by the important role of chants and organs in the churches. The intention of Islam is to represent the opposite point of view, that of dryness and sobriety in view of the "one thing needful," but it compensates this poverty by the musicality of the psalmody of the Koran, and also, in its Sufic dimension, by poetry, songs and dances, which are so many esoteric manifestations of the "wine" forbidden by exoterism; not to mention the preponderant role played by sexuality in Islam.

fact nothing other than "original sin" viewed in its Luciferian aspect. In the same way, one understands the relentlessness of the *ḥadīth* about the merchants — which we quoted first — if one takes into account the equations "avidity equals concupiscence" and "concupiscence equals fall." It is again "original sin" that is in view, but this time in its aspect of avid and avaricious egoism. Victory over "money" and "wine" becomes victory over the "old Adam": victory as such, personified by the saints and the Prophets, whose nature is none other than the *Fiṭrah*, the "primordial Nature"; that of the elect in Paradise.

The Irrefutable Religion

Again and always the confrontation Christianity-Islam; but it is an important problem, and we do not think that we have to apologize for returning to it once again.

In the face of Christianity, the argument of Islam is fundamentally — and more or less implicitly — the following. When a man knows that God is God — that He is the Supreme Reality and the Sovereign Good — and when this man stands before God with a pure heart, then he lacks nothing in regard to the essential and the decisive; he is *ḥanīf*, "pure," and fulfills the conditions required by truth and salvation. Consequently, let no one claim that this is insufficient and that man still has need of this or that; for our man stands on firm ground, no one can validly contest his double certitude: that of God and that of salvation.

It could be argued, however, that Islam also has its particular dogmas and its numerous prescriptions; this is true, but these elements are based upon the elementary conditions that we have just set forth; it is from them that these elements draw their reason for being.[1] They do not constitute the essential, although the Law must prescribe them for Moslem humanity as if they did, otherwise the essential itself would become lost.

1. Which makes us think of the following opinion of the Shaykh Al-'Alawi: all the prescriptions of the religion have as their motive the remembrance of God and nothing else.

Thus, every time man stands before God wholeheartedly — that is, "poor" and without being puffed up — he stands on the ground of absolute certitude, the certitude of his conditional salvation and the certitude of God. And that is why God has given us the gift of this supernatural key that is prayer: in order that we might stand before Him as in the primordial state, and as "always and everywhere"; or as in Eternity.

*

* *

We have said: "when man stands before God wholeheartedly." This implicitly demands that man be *bonae voluntatis:* it means, not that he must never have sinned, but that he always live with the intention of doing what brings him closer to God, while abstaining from what takes him away from God; and that he manifest this intention by his behavior; otherwise, precisely, he could not stand before God wholeheartedly.

All this is linked to the "faith which saves." Faith does not demand that man earn his salvation through given works; it demands prayer and, as a sort of prolongation of prayer, the accomplishment of one's duty, by abstention as well as action. This accomplishment, whether habitual or imposed by particular circumstances, becomes sanctified by the pre-eminent work, the first of them all, prayer; it thus participates, more or less indirectly according to its nature, in the liberating alchemy whose chief support is orison.

*

* *

In Islam and in most other religions, the Message is everything; in Christianity — and in a certain fashion also in Buddhism — it is on the contrary the Messenger who takes priority. Indeed, the great Christian argument is the fact that God Himself has come; it is this argument that is

184

meant to make Christianity at once unique and irrefutable; from the Christian standpoint, all the other Messengers seem to have been surpassed and "outclassed," and along with them their Messages. We have pointed out above that Islam remains inaccessible to this argument, by basing itself on the intrinsic truth — and the rights — of the spiritual archetypes.

If in Christianity the Messenger is all, if consequently his radiance has priority over the universal evidences we have spoken of, this is so because fundamentally the Christian perspective pertains to the mystery of immanence rather than to that of transcendence — even though it cannot avoid taking the latter mystery into account — whereas in Islam transcendence takes priority in exoterism, and immanence in esoterism. The Christian opening towards universality is not on the side of the transcendence of God, but on the side of the immanence of the Word: the entire Christian phenomenon is universalized by its interiorization, which is to say that Christ is the Word in us, that very Intellect which, according to Meister Eckhart, is "uncreated and uncreatable." Christianity projects this mystery of immanence into the dimension of transcendence, whence the concept of the Trinity which Islam, the jealous guardian of transcendentism, rejects vigorously. Be that as it may, if the irrefutability of Islam lies in the evidences founded upon the transcendent dimension of God, the irrefutability of Christianity is based on the immanent dimension, and it is through this metaphysical interpretation that the Christly phenomenon rejoins universal realities and in consequence the absolutely irrefutable truths.

In the Christian *upāya*,[2] the evidence is "existential" rather than "intellectual": the proof of this is not only the accentuation of the element "phenomenon" — namely,

---

2. Let us recall that in Buddhist terminology an *upāya* is a "celestial stratagem" meant to save us from the world of suffering, and which

the "personal coming" of God — but also and by way of consequence, the eucharistic mode; Christ is the "life" and he makes live, and one "consumes" him in the bread and wine.[3] Fundamentally, the entire evidence for the Christly phenomenon lies in this principle: "God became man that man might become God."

*

*   *

To say God is to say Salvation; God is desire to save us, as well as desire to create us. The Name of God — whatever its form — is the sign of our salvation; it is incumbent upon man not to close himself to the divine attraction. For as the Prophet-King has sung, "The Lord is my rock, and my fortress, and my deliverer."[4] And likewise Isaiah, and here it is the Eternal Himself who speaks: "I, even I, am the Lord; and beside me there is no saviour . . . there is no God else beside me; a just God and a Saviour."[5]

". . . We trust in the living God, who is the Saviour of all men, specially of those that believe."[6] This saying of the Apostle to Timothy shows the distinction between the will of God to save the believers "in fact" — these being precisely those who open themselves to Mercy — and the will to save man as such "in principle"; and this is the saving will that resides in the Divine Nature and that offers itself to all men. *Et in terra pax hominibus bonae voluntatis.*

---

can vary according to the needs of men; its "truth" is not literal, it is primarily practical or efficient.

3. In the bread, the Divinity makes Itself present and serves us as sanctifying nourishment; in the wine, It transports us out of ourselves and transforms us in order to reintegrate us into Its own Nature. At least this is so in principle and from the standpoint of potentiality, for it goes without saying that for most communicants the difference between the species remains purely virtual as regards their efficacy.

4. *II Samuel*, XXII, 2.
5. *Isaiah*, XLIII, 11 and XLV, 21.
6. *I Timothy*, IV, 10.

Part Three

The World of the Soul

Ambiguity of the Emotional Element

Not to be "emotional": this seems, nowadays, to be the very condition of "objectivity," whereas in reality objectivity is independent of the presence or absence of a sentimental element. No doubt, the word "emotional" is deservedly pejorative when emotion determines thought, or as it were creates it; that is, when emotion is the cause rather than the consequence of thought. But this same word ought to have a neutral meaning when emotion simply accompanies or stresses a correct thought; that is, when it is the consequence of thought and not its cause. It is true that a purely passional opinion may accidentally coincide with reality, but this does not invalidate the distinction we have just established.

The emotional element, when combined with a correct thought that it stresses "morally," is far from being a mere luxury, otherwise "holy wrath" would be a meaningless expression, and Christ would have been wrong in manifesting anger. Thus there are things which can and even ought to arouse indignation and contempt in the feeling soul — since the soul exists — just as there are a priori things which quite naturally arouse either respect, admiration or veneration. We say a priori, for one venerates the sacred before scorning its opposite. One loves good before hating evil, and this second attitude would not even be meaningful without the first.

189

Emotivity manifests and allows one to perceive those aspects of a good or an evil which mere logical definition could not manifest directly and concretely: these are the existential, subjective, psychological, moral and aesthetic aspects, either of truth or of error; of virtue or of vice. Let us picture a child who, through simple ignorance and thus through lack of a sense of proportions, utters a word which in fact is blasphemous; if his father thunders at him, the child "existentially" learns something which he would not have learned had the father limited himself to an abstract dissertation on the blasphemous nature of the word. The father's fulmination concretely shows the child the extent of the offense and makes visible a dimension that otherwise would have remained abstract and inoperative. The same holds true for opposite cases *mutatis mutandis:* the joy of the parents makes tangible for the child the value of his meritorious act or simply of virtue.

Contrary to experience and good sense, certain if not all practitioners of psychoanalysis consider that one must never punish a child, since they believe that punishment would "traumatize" him. What they forget is that a child who allows himself to be traumatized by a punishment that is just — and therefore proportioned to the fault — is already a monster. The essence of a normal child, in this connection, is respect for his parents and an instinct for what is good; a just punishment, far from wounding the child fundamentally, enlightens and frees him, by projecting him so to speak into the immanent awareness of the norm. Of course, there are cases in which the parents are wrong and thus the child has good reason for being traumatized. But the normal, or normally virtuous, child will not for that reason fall into a vindictive and sterile bitterness; quite the contrary: he will draw out the good from his experience, thanks to the intuition — proper to any normal person — that all adversity is metaphysically necessary, since no man can reach perfection without trials.

*

* *

Unquestionably, impassibility has its rights — to one degree or another — but it does not of itself prove the quality of objectivity; what it proves is either a legitimate intention to remain independent of some too human or too earthly *māyā* — an intention dictated by a spiritual state or a given opportuneness or simply by the proportions of things — or else, on the contrary, it proves an insolent ostentation, hence pride or stupidity. If natural dignity requires a certain impassibility — thereby manifesting the "motionless mover" and the sense of the sacred — it does not, however, exclude the natural impulses of the soul, as is shown by the lives of the sages and saints, and above all by everyday experience.

This is not to say that the emotion of a spiritual man is altogether like that of a profane man; the very term "holy wrath" shows that in a spiritual man a sanctifying element is present which is lacking in a profane man, namely an underlying serenity which prolongs, so to speak, "the motionless mover," and which stems — in Eckhartian terminology — from the "inner man," whereas emotion as such is situated in the "outer man." In a spiritual man there is continuity between his inward impassibility — resulting from consciousness of the Immutable — and his emotion: when a spiritual man becomes angry, it is so to speak on the basis of his contemplative impassibility and not in a manner contrary to it, whereas a profane man becomes totally enclosed in his anger, and this to the very extent that the anger is unjust or disproportionate; he "becomes enclosed," that is, cut off from his consciousness of God, hence from his substance of immortality. It is in this sense — and in this sense only — that theology considers anger to be a mortal sin, without however overlooking that there is a holy anger which reflects and prolongs the Divine Anger. Emotion is profane to the extent that it be-

191

longs to man alone, in which case the celestial Archetype cannot enter into play.

All this shows that in the emotion of a spiritual man, the "motionless mover" always remains present and accessible. As his emotion is linked to knowledge, the truth is never betrayed; his mind remains lucid, spontaneously and without pedantry.

*

* *

On the one hand, we rightly admire something because we understand it; on the other hand, we understand something admirable in admiring it, which is to say that our admiration widens and deepens our initial comprehension. Emotion or sentiment in this case is a mode of assimilation;[1] it is thus a subordinate mode of knowledge, which logically intervenes *a posteriori,* but which in fact may coincide with physical or intellectual perception. Thus nobleness of character, or virtue, is primarily a predisposition to quasi-existential adequation, parallel to knowledge properly so called; it is a manner of being objective, of being in conformity with reality and, according to the case, it will require a certain abnegation, for to be perfectly objective is to die a little, as we have written elsewhere.

Nowadays, one praises the "objectivity" of a man who calmly and coolly asserts that two and two make five, whereas the man who indignantly replies that two and two make four[2] is accused of subjectivity or of being emotional. One does not wish to admit that objectivity is

---

1. Which brings us to the principle: *Credo ut intelligam.*
2. There is a popular French saying: "He gets angry, thus he is wrong," which is always applied the wrong way round. In reality, this saying refers to people who become angry because, being wrong, they run short of arguments; anger thus makes up for the lack of proof and of right.

adequation to the object and not a manner of speaking; that the criterion of objectivity is reality and not the tone or the facial expression; nor above all a sham, inhuman and insolent placidity. Also, and above all, one forgets that emotion has its rights in the arsenal of human dialectic, and that these rights could not be contrary to objectivity. Even the most strictly objective thought — whether intellectual or rational — is accompanied by a psychic, hence subjective, factor, namely the sentiment of certitude, without which man would not be man. Now man is "made in the image of God"; this is the very reason for his being. To blame man for a natural and fundamental characteristic amounts to blaming not only the creative intention, but the very Nature of the Creator.

Anti-emotional and artificially impassible "objectivism" betrays its falseness by the following contradiction: those who make themselves the spokesmen of an imperturbable and impertinent rationality are at the same time those who proclaim free love — they have no taste for asceticism — or who flare up as soon as one speaks of politics — to mention some inconsequentialities among others. This proves that their "objectivity" is no more than error and ostentation, and is related to pride and bitterness; from which comes the propensity to whitewash vile men — unless they happen to be political adversaries — and to blacken men of good will, calmly and without passion, at least without visible passion; this being just one example of that one-sided morality so characteristic of all kinds of hypocrisy. Be that as it may, one has to react against the widespread psychoanalytical opinion that indignation as well as enthusiasm always reveal prejudice or partiality; this simplistic opinion is related to another, no less stupid, error, namely that in an argument no one is ever altogether right, and that whoever becomes angry is always wrong.

It is important to be aware of the way words are used: when the terms "objectivity" and "subjectivity," or "rationality" and "sentimentality" are juxtaposed in the sense of a qualitative opposition, it goes without saying that the second term is pejorative, since it is supposed to denote a privation; but it is not pejorative in itself, for it refers a priori to a phenomenon which in itself is neutral, hence possibly qualitative. No doubt, the conventions of language do not allow us to treat "subjectivity" or "emotivity" as a quality, as they do with "objectivity" or "rationality"; on the contrary, when we wish to express the positive aspect of sentiment, these conventions oblige us to specify the content, thus to speak of "nobleness of character" or of "virtue," virtue being the complement of "truth." Sentiment in conformity to truth is by that very fact noble and virtuous; nobleness is an adequation, as we have said before; there is nothing arbitrary in it, contrary to the case of sentiments that are inadequate or disproportionate and thereby opposed to beauty of soul.

No doubt, the loftiest ideas, above all metaphysical truths, do not necessarily entail emotions properly so called; but they necessarily confer upon the soul of the knowing subject the sentiment of certitude, and also serenity, peace and joy.[3] Fundamentally, we would say that where there is Truth, there also is Love. Each *Deva* possesses its *Shakti;* in the human microcosm, the feeling soul is joined to the discerning intellect,[4] as in the Divine Order Mercy is joined to Omniscience; and as, in the final analysis, Infinitude is consubstantial with the Absolute.

---

3. In Islamic language, knowledge in fact brings about a "dilation" (*inshirāh*).

4. "It is not good that the man should be alone," says Genesis. And let us recall that there is no *jñāna* without an element of *bhakti*.

194

The Psychological Imposture

What we term "psychological imposture" is the tendency to reduce everything to psychological factors and to call into question not only what is intellectual or spiritual — the first being related to truth and the second to life in and by truth — but also the human spirit as such, and therewith its capacity of adequation and, still more evidently, its inward illimitation and transcendence. The same belittling and truly subversive tendency rages in all the domains that "scientism" claims to embrace, but its most acute expression is beyond all doubt to be found in psychoanalysis. Psychoanalysis is at once an endpoint and a cause, as is always the case with profane ideologies, like materialism and evolutionism, of which it is really a logical and fatal ramification and a natural ally.

Psychoanalysis doubly deserves to be classed as an imposture, firstly because it pretends to have discovered facts which have always been known and could never have been otherwise than known, and secondly and chiefly because it arrogates to itself functions that in reality are spiritual, and thus poses practically as a religion. What is called "examination of conscience" or, by the Moslems, "the science of humors" *('ilm al-khawāṭir)*, or "investigation" *(vichara)* by the Hindus — with a rather different slant in each case — is nothing other than an objective analysis of the near and distant causes of ways of acting and reacting that we repeat automatically without being aware of their real motives, or without discerning the real character of those motives. It may happen that a man habitually, and blindly, commits the same errors in the same circumstances, because he carries within himself, in his subconscious, traumas or errors founded on conceit. To be healed, he must detect these complexes and translate them into clear formulas; he must become conscious of subconscious errors and neutralize them by means of contrary affirmations. If he succeeds, his virtues will be all the more lucid. It is in this sense that Lao Tsu said: "To feel an illness is to have it no longer"; and the Law of Manu says: "There is no lustral water that compares with knowledge," that is, with objectification by the intelligence.

What is new in psychoanalysis, and what gives it its sinister originality, is its determination to attribute every reflex and every disposition of the soul to mean causes and to exclude spiritual factors; hence its notorious tendency to see health in what is commonplace and vulgar, and neurosis in what is noble and profound. Man cannot escape in this world from trials and temptations; his soul is therefore inevitably stamped with some sort of turmoil, unless it be of an angelic serenity, which may occur in all religious surroundings, or, on the contrary, unless it be of an unshakable inertia, which occurs everywhere. But psychoanalysis, instead of allowing man to make the best of his natural, and in a sense providential, disequilibrium — and the best is whatever is profitable to his ultimate destiny — tends on the contrary to bring him back to an amorphous equilibrium, rather as if one wished to spare a young bird the agonies of apprenticeship by clipping its wings. Analogically speaking: if a man is distressed by a flood and seeks a way to escape from it, psychoanalysis would remove the distress and let the patient drown; or again, instead of abolishing sin, it abolishes the sense of guilt, thus allowing the patient to go serenely to hell. This is not to say that it never happens that a psychoanalyst discovers and dissolves a dangerous complex without at the same time ruining the patient; but we are here concerned with the principle, in which the perils and errors involved infinitely outweigh the contingent advantages and fragmentary truths.

As a result, for the average psychoanalyst a complex is bad because it is a complex; he refuses to see that there are complexes which do honor to man or are natural to him by virtue of his deiformity, and consequently that there are disequilibriums that are necessary, and that must be resolved from above ourselves and not from beneath.[1] There is another error that is fundamentally the same: it is to regard an equilibrium as good because it is an equilibrium, as if there were no equilibriums made of insensibility or of perversion. Our human state itself is a disequilibrium, since we are existentially suspended between earthly contingencies and the inborn summons of the Absolute; to get rid of a psychic knot is not the whole question, one must also know how and why it should be gotten rid of. We are not amorphous substances, we are movements which are in principle ascensional; our happiness must be proprotioned to our total nature, on pain of lowering us to animality, for a happiness without God is precisely what man cannot withstand without becoming lost. And that is why a physician of the soul must be a *pontifex*, and thus a spiritual master in the proper and traditional sense of the word. A profane professional has neither the capacity nor, consequently, the right to interfere with the soul beyond such elementary difficulties as simple common sense can resolve.

The spiritual and social crime of psychoanalysis is therefore its usurpation of the place of religion or of the wisdom that is the wisdom of God, and the elimination from its procedures of all consideration of our ultimate destiny. It is as if, being unable to fight against God, one were to attack the human soul which belongs to Him and is des-

---

1. ". . . for it is profitable for thee that one of thy members should perish, and not that thy whole body should be cast into hell." *(Matthew, V, 29)*.

197

tined for Him, by debasing the divine image instead of its Prototype. Like every solution that avoids the supernatural, psychoanalysis replaces in its own way what it abolishes: the void it produces by its intentional or unintentional destructions expands it, and condemns it to postulate a false infinite or to function as a pseudo-religion.

In order to develop, psychoanalysis needed a favorable soil, not only from the point of view of ideas, but also from that of psychological phenomena. What this means is that the Europeans, who have always been of a cerebral type, have become infinitely more so in the last two centuries, approximately. Now, this concentration of the whole intelligence in the head is something excessive and abnormal, and the hypertrophies to which it gives rise do not constitute a superiority, despite their efficacy in certain domains.

Normally the intelligence ought to reside, not in the mind alone, but also in the heart, and it should also be spread throughout the body, as is especially the case with men who are called "primitive" but who are undeniably superior in certain respects. Be that as it may, the point we wish to make is that psychoanalysis is to a great extent the result of a mental disequilibrium more or less generally prevalent in a world in which the machine dictates to man the rhythm of his life, and, what is more serious still, even of his soul and his spirit.

*

* *

Psychoanalysis has effected a more or less official entry into the world of "believers," which is indeed a sign of the times. This has led to the introduction into so-called "spirituality" of a method totally incompatible with human dignity, and at the same time strangely contradicting the pretension of being "adult" and "emancipated." People play at being demigods and at the same time treat themselves as irresponsibles; for the slightest depression, caused either by too hectic an ambience, or by a manner of life far

198

too contrary to good sense, people rush off to the psychiatrist, whose work will consist in instilling in them some false optimism or in recommending some "liberating" sin. Nobody seems to have even an inkling of the fact that there is but one equilibrium, namely that which fixes us in our real center and in God.

One of the most odious effects of the adoption of the psychoanalytical approach by believers is the disfavoring of the cult of the Holy Virgin; only a barbarous mentality that wants to be "adult" at all costs and no longer believes in anything but the trivial could be embarassed by this cult. The answer to the reproach of "gynecolatry" or of "Oedipus complex" is that, like every other psychoanalytical argument, it by-passes the problem; for the real question is not what the psychological conditioning of an attitude may be, but on the contrary, what its results are. When for instance one is told that someone has chosen metaphysics as an "escape" or a "sublimation" and because of an "inferiority complex" or a "refusal to look facts in the face," all this is of no importance whatever, for blessed be the complex that is the occasional cause of an acceptance of the true and the good! But there is also this: the moderns, tired as they are of the artificial softness with which their culture and their religiosity have been loaded since the baroque period, extend their aversion — as is their habit — to all legitimate sweetness and delicacy, and thus shut themselves off, either from an entire spiritual dimension, if they are "believers," or even from all genuine humanity, as is shown by a certain infantile cult of coarseness and noise.

And besides, it is not enough to ask what a particular devotion is worth in particular souls, one must also ask what is to replace it; for the place of a suppressed devotion never remains empty.

*

* *

"Know thyself" (Hellenism) says Tradition, and also "He who knoweth his own soul knoweth his Lord" (Islam). The traditional model of what psychoanalysis ought to be, or claims to be, is the science of virtues and vices; the fundamental virtue is sincerity and it coincides with humility; one who plunges the probe of truth and rectitude into his soul ends by detecting the subtlest knots of the unconscious. It is useless to seek to heal the soul without healing the spirit; what matters in the first place is to clear the intelligence of the errors perverting it, and thus create a foundation in view of the soul's return to equilibrium; not to just any equilibrium, but to the equilibrium whose principle the soul bears within itself.

St. Bernard said that the passionate soul is a "contemptible thing," and Meister Eckhart enjoins us to "hate" it. This means that the great remedy for all our inward miseries is objectivity towards ourselves; and the source or starting point of this objectivity is situated above ourselves, in God. That which is in God is for that reason mirrored in our own transpersonal center which is the pure Intellect; that is, the Truth that saves us is part of our most intimate and most real substance. Error, or impiety, is the refusal to be what one is.

Anonymity of the Virtues

According to Saint Augustine, "all the other vices attach themselves to evil, that it may be done; only pride attaches itself to good, that it may perish." And likewise the Curé d'Ars: "Humility is to the virtues what the string is to the rosary; remove the string and all the beads scatter; remove humility and all the virtues disappear." In other words, pride consists in glorying in one's virtues, either before others or before oneself. And this destroys the virtues for two reasons: first of all because one takes them away from God, to whom they belong in reality, thus putting oneself — like Lucifer — in place of the Divine Source; and secondly because one attributes *de facto* a disproportionate value to a phenomenon which is necessarily relative. "When thou givest alms, let not thy left hand know what thy right hand doeth."

It has been mistakenly concluded that a virtuous man has no awareness of his virtues, and that to be aware of them is pride. Now the fact that someone who is proud readily attributes to himself all the virtues he can conceive of, in no way implies that every man who is aware of his virtues is proud, for not all awarenesses are alike. Man, being "made in the image of God," has the gift of intelligence; to say intelligence is to say objectivity, which implies that the thesis — whether philosophical or moralistic — of the fundamental subjectivity of man is a contradiction pure and simple; for whoever is deprived of objectiv-

201

ity can ascertain nothing whatsoever, not even that he is subjective.[1] Man endowed with objectivity possesses by that very fact the faculty of looking at himself as if he were another. If we must admit that others have qualities — and humility demands that we do so — we cannot deny the possibility of having them ourselves; if, on the contrary, we must piously believe that we are not capable of any good, we must also believe it of others. In any case, a humble person is not attached to attributing virtue to himself personally; he is attached to virtue for its own sake, to virtue as such; not so that he may possess it, but because it is beautiful; and being beautiful, it necessarily belongs to the Sovereign Good.

It may be asked: what is the equation "intelligence equals pride" founded upon? If it meant that a purely mental — not "cardiac" or "intellective" — intelligence risks succumbing to the profane and worldly temptation of an autocratic luciferism, then the equation would be correct; but it is wrong not to specify this and thus give the impression that ingelligence is prideful in itself, which is a contradiction in terms. No doubt the equation at issue fulfills the function of waging a preventive war against a rationalism that is hostile to faith; which is an excuse but not a justification.

Let us return now to the question of moral qualities: as every virtue by definition comprises a beatitude, even the humblest of men cannot help enjoying a good conscience — unless they deprive themselves of it because of some unrealistic, but possibly efficacious, mystical zeal; nor can they help knowing a priori that we necessarily possess in a relative manner that which God has bestowed upon us and which He alone possesses in an absolute manner; for even if a value belongs to us because God has bestowed it upon us — so that we actually possess it on our

---

1. The thesis of the subjectivity of the human spirit destroys the very definition of man.

own level — it nevertheless belongs to Him entirely, since no value can be situated outside the Sovereign Good. One could say that man enters into virtue as he would enter into a sanctuary, and that virtue expels the ambitious who claim it for themselves.

Moreover, a man who is both humble and intelligent can feel often enough that he has virtues, but he will always know that he does not dispose of God's measures; he knows that our situation as earthly men does not allow us to rest on the all too precarious awareness of our qualities. For there is always the distinction between the Absolute and the relative, and thus the sense of proportions; no intelligent man can escape these functions of the spirit.

*

* *

Strictly speaking, man must not wish to "acquire" this or that virtue, he must wish to eliminate this or that vice. To realize a quality, is to destroy the fault contrary to it, given the fact that what is primordial is normal and that the primordial precedes the fall and decadence. This truth brings us to the following consideration: there are men who have the vainglorious ambition to be particularly intelligent, and this makes them all the more stupid; their case would not be hopeless if they had the good sense and humility to recognize their limits — for which Heaven could not reproach them — and if they took their stand modestly on wholesome, and thus intelligent, principles. A mirror has no need of ornaments, it needs purity; ornament in this case amounts to an "ideal" which is both individualistic and perfectionistic, while purity refers to the exigencies of the real. Now, like the mirror, our intention should be conformable to its object with respect to essence and efficacy, and not merely with respect to form. It is true that intelligence is not a virtue, but an extra-moral quality or more precisely a faculty, a distinction which makes however no difference from the standpoint that interests us here; all the more so since intelligence is closely combined with virtue to the extent that it remains faithful to its innermost nature which is "objectivity," and hence detachment and impartiality. To be entirely objective is to die a little.

In a certain metaphysical sense, only our faults belong to us; our qualities belong to God, to the Good as such. By eliminating the vices, we allow God's qualities to penetrate our soul; from another point of view — as we mentioned above — it is we who enter into virtue. Obviously, the merit of virtue eludes someone who believes that "I am virtue"; to be conscious of a virtue is one thing, to be self-satisfied with this consciousness is another.

We could also express ourselves as follows: every man likes to be out in the light and fresh air; no one would like to be shut up in a dark, airless tower; and that is how one should love the virtues, and detest the vices. No man who enjoys light and air would think of proclaiming "I am the sun," or "I am the sky"; one loves an ambience which is light and airy, and that is why one enters it. And that is how one should enter the virtues: because they are self-evident by their nature and because one loves their climate.

A proud man who is reproached for a fault, either denies it, or else minimizes it while eventually assuming responsibility for it, saying with a cynical individualism "but I am made that way"; an attitude which is fundamentally diabolical, since God alone has the right to say: "I am that I am." A proud man either denies his faults, or is proud of them; the corollary of this attitude is that he exaggerates the faults of others. He even projects his own faults — without minimizing them in this case — into others, including those who have not the slightest trace of them; and with these he does it more especially so, out of a kind of vengeance.

A humble man, on the contrary, does not believe that he has a right to have a fault, all the more so as he does not believe that he has faults which are interesting and lova-

204

ble. A humble man would rather be a beggar out in the light and fresh air than a king in a dark, airless tower; and he would not dream of saying either that darkness is light, or that he is the light. Of course, a proud man may have natural qualities, but one should never excuse pride on account of them; for man has no right to love what is unacceptable to God.

*
* *

In order to overcome a fault, one has to make use of all that one has and all that one is: intelligence, will, and sentiment. By this last word we mean the capacity to love, which also implies the capacity to hate; the sense of the beautiful necessarily implies the sense of the ugly, since we live in a world of contrasts or of contrasting manifestation. Likewise, no one can venerate if he does not have the capacity to despise.[2] Evidently, there is a metaphysical or mystical point of view which transcends all differences and which considers phenomena only with respect to their mere existence, their character of divine manifestation, or of *māyā*, but this point of view cannot legitimately apply in all situations; one has to know how to put each thing in its proper place.

Intelligence informs us of the cosmic significance of the virtues and also of their human necessity, both individual and social; it shows us their obvious value and at the same time the absurdity of the vices. Sentiment — the feeling soul — convinces us through beauty; as for will, it puts into practice both our sense of the beautiful and our comprehension of the true. This means that to overcome a

---

2. If one had to love and admire everything, as for example certain dreamers of a more or less Buddhist cast would have it, the fulminations of the *Magnificat* or of the Sermon on the Mount would be inexplicable. Charity or "compassion" is not flabbiness, apart from the fact that charity may require hardness.

fault one has, first of all, to understand its nature; secondly, to detest it in consequence, and thirdly, to put this comprehension and this disposition into practice. Now to understand the nature of a fault is above all to understand the nature of the virtue it denies; likewise, hatred of evil is only conceivable in relation to the good it excludes and in relation to the love of this good. It is knowledge and love which give wings to will; it is not so difficult to want something when we understand its self-evidence and its necessity, and when in addition we love it and consequently detest its absence or opposite.

If in fact we are saints, that is of interest to Heaven since Heaven is interested in our spiritual welfare; but our individualistic and perfectionistic desire for holiness is of no interest to it. We may pray and ask God to free us from a fault — on condition that we neglect nothing that will help free us from it — but we may not ask God to make us perfect. One should overcome a fault in order to rid the world of it rather than with the intention of adorning oneself with a quality. Doubtless the desire to be perfect is not lacking in logic, but the desire not to be imperfect is more realistic and more concrete, and also more modest.

Nothing can be accomplished without the aid of Heaven; now Heaven has given us the capacity to think, to will and to love. The Spirit became flesh that the flesh might become Spirit.

Passion and Pride

In the fallen nature of man there is a double infirmity and, spiritually speaking, a double obstacle: on the one hand passion, which draws man outside himself while at the same time compressing him, and on the other hand pride, which shuts man within himself, while at the same time dispersing him. Passion reveals itself by attachment, and pride by ambition; even if the latter were spiritual, it still would be worldly, unless one were to give the word ambition — as is sometimes done — a transposed and neutral meaning. In an analogous way, if one understands by the word passion a force in itself neutral and of potential value one can evidently speak of holy passions, or passions sanctified by their object; but it is obviously not this conversion of a natural energy that is in question when we speak here of infirmities or obstacles. In this connection it must be pointed out that pride does not admit of such a conversion; it can only be destroyed or dissolved — the first term indicating a privative or penitential ascesis and the second an alchemy of love able to "melt the heart" — depending upon the degrees or modes of hardness. It is true that one can sometimes speak of "legitimate pride," but this is situated on an inoffensive plane having nothing to do with vice or sin.

Passion, as it is to be understood here, is to prefer the world to God; pride is to prefer oneself to God or, metaphysically speaking, to prefer sensory consciousness to the immanent Self. Or again, to paraphrase the words of a saint: passion is to flee from God, pride is to rise up against Him. In consequence, one can say that to prefer the world — in the form of some thing — to truth or to good, is passion; to prefer oneself — in the form of some vanity — to truth or to good, is pride; for truth, or good, is the trace of God and represents God.

Passion expresses itself not only by attachment, but also, and in a more pernicious way, by insatiability. Pride expresses itself not only by ambition, it is yet more vicious when it takes the form of obstinacy. And this shows that the two vices necessarily intermingle: obstinate passion does not go without a measure of pride; insatiable pride does not go without a measure of passion. A man who is without any pride will also be without passion, and he who is wholly without passion will also be without pride.

A prideful man may have all the virtues, even some humility, but he arrogates them to his person and thus illusorily cuts them off from God, thereby taking away all their intrinsic value and profound efficacy; which means that the virtues of a prideful man are as it were deprived of their content. As for a humble man, he is well aware that the virtues belong to him on loan, just as light belongs in a certain way to the water which reflects it, but he never loses sight of the fact that he is not the author of his virtues — any more than the water is the source of the light — and that the finest virtues are nothing apart from God. Conversely, even if one tries to separate them from God in order to appropriate them to oneself, whatever value they may retain still belongs to God.

A man may have a sincere desire for humility — thus for objectivity towards himself — and may realize thereby a mode of true humility, but at the same time cannot bear any humiliation, even if merited or innocuous. In this case his humility is compromised to a greater or lesser extent by an element of pride, which will also manifest itself by a certain propensity to humiliate others, even if it be only in underestimating them and in interpreting unfavorably something susceptible of a favorable interpretation. That a mixture of humility and pride can exist proves that pride, like passion, comprises degrees: in fact it is necessary to distinguish between a vice that is in the very substance of a man and another that is only an accident; the accidental is capable of being remedied, the substantial is not.

We have just seen that a criterion of pride — of a pride which is perhaps only accidental and not fundamental — is the propensity to brook no humiliations while readily inflicting them upon others. The right attitude is not to rebel against a humiliation when it manifests the truth, and to accept willingly humiliations which do not involve our true dignity, that which God has conferred upon us by His creative act and which is an extension of His own. Nothing harms our dignity as "image of God" as much as pride, because it cuts us off from the divine substance of our dignity. We are well aware that from a certain ascetic and sentimental point of view no humiliation is unmerited, but that is a question of method and not of norm, whereas our perspective is based on the nature of things and not on a voluntarist and emotional automatism.

There are prideful people who appear humble because they avoid disparaging others while being nevertheless steeped in their own importance, as there are on the contrary those who seem humble because they make little of their own worth while nevertheless underestimating others. Or again there are people who are considered humble because they seem so before God, or before the spiritual master, or before one of the great of this world, whereas they are not at all humble before their peers, which proves precisely that they are sincerely humble neither towards their superiors nor towards God.

Attachment, selfishness and insatiability belong to passion; ambition, pretension and obstinacy to pride. The two vices, pride and passion, may have stupidity and mal-

209

ice in common, apart from the fact that all the vices share in an indirect solidarity.

*

* *

It is not without reason that popular opinion tends to associate pride with stupidity. One can in fact be pretentious through stupidity just as one can be stupid through pretension; the two things go together. Of course, lack of intelligence does not necessarily lead to pretension, but pretension cannot avoid harming the intelligence. And if, as is commonly admitted, stupidity is the incapacity to discern between the essential and the secondary, or between cause and effect, it includes for that very reason a measure of pride; a stupidity combined with a perfect humility and a perfect detachment would no longer be stupidity, it would be a simplicity of mind which could trouble no intelligent and virtuous person.

Closely related to pretension is self-satisfaction, with the difference that it is passive, while pretension is active. The self-satisfied person is not one who with good reason and complete humility is conscious of the worth of what he knows or does, but rather one who is saturated with his own imaginary worth which he projects onto his scanty knowledge and mediocre activity. Humility, for its part, is in no wise contrary to authority, and could not be so since authority is a positive quality; humility is not modesty, by which we mean that authority excludes modesty while nonetheless including humility. Setting aside all humilitarianism — automatic and extravagant as it may be, though inevitable and efficacious in the psychological order corresponding to it — humility is the awareness of our real, and not imaginary, littleness in its various aspects, together with the absence of all desire for individual affirmation. Modesty, on the contrary, is the awareness, not of our ontological limitation or of our human insufficiency, but simply of our incompetence or our incapacity, as the case may be. Thus on the one hand modesty resembles humility, yet on the other hand differs from it, and this may be illustrated by saying that a modest man must of necessity be humble, but a humble man need not necessarily be modest.

*
* *

There is a certain *de facto* relationship, humanly speaking, between passion and beauty, as likewise between pride and intelligence: for fallen man beauty and intelligence have become two-edged swords, which explains the ostracism they often suffer at the hands of moralists, even at the level of theology. In esoterism, however, intelligence and beauty are thoroughly restored to their real standing and value, for by definition esoterism considers the aseity of things and not their opportuneness on some lower plane; it has always recognized that things which for some can be a seduction and a cause of perdition, can for others be a call to God; herein lies the whole mystery of the metaphysical transparency of phenomena.

Setting aside the weakness of human nature, or the intangible factors of this weakness, as the case may be, the truth of the matter is simple: intelligence and beauty are intrinsically positive. But extrinsically and practically, they are positive or good only on the express condition that, subjectively, they not be separated from God; and that, objectively, they not be envisaged apart from God, and in the end as counter to God, as was precisely the case with classical Greece and the Renaissance, under the double aspect of thought and art.

*
* *

To passion, the things of this world appear in some way absolute; to pride, it is the ego that takes on this appearance. Now, this is obviously incompatible, not only with

211

the concept of God, but even more so with the practices of meditation and realization that pertain thereto. To combine the idolatry and the narcissism of man's fallen nature with practices converging on the Infinite — relating to Immanence as well as to Transcendence — is assuredly the most flagrant of hypocrisies and the most fatal of absurdities.

It follows from nearly all our preceding considerations that our point of view is not that of individual and sentimental voluntarism: it coincides neither with penitentialism, according to which only the disagreeable leads to God, nor with humilitarianism, according to which every man should think himself the greatest of all sinners. In speaking of passion and attachment, we do not mean a natural attachment to certain things that every man can experience and that is in no way opposed to the sense of relativity or to serenity of spirit, or to detachment generally; we have solely in mind the passional attachment which places an absolute value on relative things to the detriment of the love of God. And in speaking of pride, ambition and pretension, we do not mean natural self-respect, or the awareness which the most objective man may have of his worth, or the sense of dignity or honor — none of these is in any way opposed to the awareness of our metaphysical nothingness or to true humility in relation to others. We have solely in mind overestimation of oneself, which is inevitably accompanied by underestimation of others and which for that very reason renders sincere effacement before God impossible. Pride is the desire to "keep one's life"; it is the refusal to "die before one dies."

*

* *

Psychologically or morally speaking, there is a distinction between men who are proud and others who are not, whatever the degree of the vice. In volitive and sentimental mysticism one would say on the contrary that every man is proud, which on the one hand is false — for then the words would practically be devoid of meaning — but which on the other hand is nonetheless true in relation to the virtuality of pride to be found in every man and which can be actualized according to circumstances, even if only to a slight degree. Mystical voluntarism seeks to cut short all ineffective subtlety; spiritual intellectuality, however, operates by means of truth and not by means of zeal, consequently the remedy it employs will not be a useful and leveling approximation, but a precise knowledge of the malady. A gnostic — in the original and not sectarian sense of the word — does not ask: "What attitude of will and sentiment is the most contrary to pride?" but rather: "What in this particular case is the nature of things, and what consequently is the positive attitude — of the spirit and the soul — of which pride is the negation or the privation?" First, the attitude of the spirit: namely, discernment between the Absolute and the relative, and in the relative between the essential and the secondary — discernment which entails *ipso facto* the sanctifying and unitive contemplation of the Absolute and of the essential. Then the attitude of the soul, itself governed by this discernment or by this sense of proportion and equilibrium: namely, self-effacement on the one hand, and generosity on the other; for all the fundamental virtues are included in these two qualities.

Effacement towards God first and then, as a consequence of this vertical quality, effacement towards the world, thus in the horizontal dimension: all virtue and all merit come from God, we are merely reverberating facets. A perspicacious and virtuous man, aware that he cannot in any fashion or in any respect add his personal qualities to the Divine Perfection — the only one there is — and that consequently he is nothing before God but a pauper, would not wish to vaunt himself before men either; in other words, he would not think of imposing or putting forward his person as such. He would exercise his function, he would perform his duty, he might perhaps be king, but it would not be his individual person that he would affirm, even if his function obliged him to impose his person as agent and symbol: kings and pontiffs receive in an impersonal manner, and in humbleness before God, the honors due to them. A humble man does not derive any pleasure or any ambition from the fact of being "I," and he has no prejudice with regard to "others."

And the same for generosity: it must be exercised first towards God and then towards men. Everyone knows what generosity is with regard to the neighbor: but what is it with regard to God? It is the gift of oneself in contemplation, and — to the extent that this is possible — extinction in the Divine Life in the depth of our hearts.

What matters for man and what decides his ultimate destiny is his spiritual Knowledge, his faith, his character and his activity. Now the foundation of a noble character is precisely self-effacement and generosity: self-effacement or poverty, which implies detachment, sobriety, patience and contentment; and generosity or magnanimity, which implies fervor, perseverance, trust and joy in God.

Passion and pride constitute a priori the flaw and the obstacle; mingled with the highest spiritual aspirations, they become an abomination. We will be told that this has always been known, because it is evident; that may be. But the things that have never been unknown seem to be at the same time those that men have the greatest difficulty in learning.

214

Trials and Happiness

Since evil is inevitable in the world, it is inevitable also in one's destiny; being necessary in the economy of the objective reality surrounding us, it is no less necessary in the experience of the subject-witness; the imperfections of the world are coupled with the trials of life.

First of all one has to answer the question of why the painful experiences that man must undergo are called "trials." We would reply that these experiences are trials in relation to our faith, which indicates that with regard to troubling or painful experiences we have duties resulting from our human vocation. In other words, we must prove our faith in relation to God and and in relation to ourselves; in relation to God, by our intelligence, our sense of absoluteness, and thus our sense of relativities and proportions; and in relation to ourselves, by our character, our resignation to destiny, our gratitude. There are in fact two ways to conquer the traces that evil, or more precisely suffering, leaves in the soul. These are, firstly: our awareness of the Sovereign Good, which coincides with our hope to the extent that this awareness penetrates us; and secondly: our acceptance of what, in religious language, is called the "will of God." And assuredly it is a great victory over oneself to accept a destiny because it is God's will and for no other reason.

Life is a chain of moments, and we can — and must — at every moment say "yes" to the divine Will; that is, to what God wills for us at this very moment. Doubtless this does not deliver us from the evils we must face in the outward world, but it does deliver us from our passional reactions to these evils. Without our knowing or willing it, these reactions — made of bitterness or even despair — are revolts against divine decrees, and that is why, quite often, God is slow to save us from our tribulations. The error here is, on the one hand, wishing the world to be other than what it is, and on the other hand, wishing that what happens to us were not our destiny.

The golden rule is, firstly: to resign oneself to the will of God as it is manifested in the inevitable, although we are obviously free — and even obliged, according to case — to suppress avoidable evil if we can do so justly. And secondly: to trust in the Justice and Goodness of God and place our cares in His hands, while accomplishing with equity what we can or must accomplish, for "Heaven helps those who help themselves."

A trial is not necessarily a chastisement, it can also be a grace, and the one does not preclude the other. At all events: a trial in itself not only tests what we are, but also purifies us of what we are not.

But there is also holy gratitude; by this we mean our awareness of the divine gifts that enable us to live and that, out of simple habit, we have forgotten. Gratitude — the capacity to appreciate even little things — forms part of nobleness of soul, as does generosity; both virtues help us, together with faith, to bear the burdens that destiny imposes upon us. God helps us to bear our burdens when we bear them with faith and magnanimity.

We have to beware of becoming hypnotized by the surrounding world, for this reinforces our feeling of being exposed to a thousand dangers. It is as if one were walking along a narrow path between two abysses: when looking to either side one risks losing one's balance; one must, on the contrary, look straight ahead and let the world be the world. The whole purpose of our life lies before us, and that is one of the meanings of the injunction not to look behind when one has put one's hand to the plow. It is necessary to look towards God, in relation to Whom all the chasms of the world are nothing.

*

* *

Independently of the trials of life which concern our faith and our moral perfection, there are ritual and initiatory trials which refer to our superior spiritual qualifications; they are met with in the Egyptian and Greco-Roman mysteries of Antiquity and later, in the artisanal initiations of Christian Europe. On the one hand, these are symbolical actions representing various aspects of the cosmic *māyā* which the neophyte is supposed to vanquish within himself; on the other hand, they are "touchstones" intended to provoke in the neophyte reactions that test his qualification, or his disqualification, for surpassing himself. The initiatory way by definition implies operations that risk bringing about disequilibriums and falls; thus it is necessary to prevent those who do not fulfill the requisite conditions from committing themselves. But this does not mean that these ritual trials are found wherever there is an initiation and a corresponding method, for there are other means to try our capacities, or to cushion psychic shocks, if need be. These means are above all of the moral order, whereas in the ancient and artisanal mysteries they are rather of the "alchemical" order, so to speak.

The most important or characteristic initiatory trials are perhaps the "trial by water" and the "trial by fire." The first seems to refer to the gentle and seductive *māyā*, and the second to the terrible and destructive *māyā*: it is necessary to brave not only the "sirens' song" but also the "dragons." Both powers sleep within ourselves and awaken as soon as we seek to go beyond their level; but they exist a priori in the macrocosm, of which we are part and which we realize in individual and subjective mode. In spiritual combat, both *māyās*, the outward and the inward, combine to create obstacles. But there is also the celestial *Māyā*, most often represented by a goddess — in Christianity by the Holy Virgin — who comes to the aid of the combatant, on condition that he has taken the measures, or fulfilled the conditions, that allow the celestial *Māyā* to intervene.

*

* *

One of the first conditions of happiness is the renunciation of the superficial and habitual need to feel happy. But this renunciation cannot spring from the void; it must have a meaning, and this meaning cannot but come from above, from what constitutes our reason for being. In fact, for too many men, the criterion of the value of life is a passive feeling of happiness which a priori is determined by the outer world; when this feeling does not occur or when it fades — which may have subjective as well as objective causes — they become alarmed, and are as if possessed by the question: "Why am I not happy as I was before?" and by the awaiting of something that could give them the feeling of being happy. All this, it is unnecessary to stress, is a perfectly worldly attitude, hence incompatible with the least of spiritual perspectives. To become enclosed in an earthly happiness is to create a barrier between man and Heaven, and it is to forget that on earth man is in exile; the very fact of death proves it.

The first response to the profane expectation of the feeling of happiness or to the bad habit of imprisoning oneself in this expectation as if there were not above us a boundless and serene sky — the first response then, is the remembrance of the Sovereign Good, or in other words, the awareness of its Reality and its Bliss. It is this awareness that allows us to perceive the relativity and pettiness of our "complex" of happiness, and to ascertain that in this expectation there are two fundamental vices, namely concupiscence and idolatry; two things, therefore, which take us away from God, and consequently from Felicity as such, the source of all happiness.

But there is something else: to the renunciation we have spoken of above, there should be joined what can most simply be called the "life of prayer." One has to be able to find happiness in the spiritual act, the gift of self, rather than in the passive and narcissistic enjoyment of a well-being that the world is supposed to offer us. "It is more blessed to give than to receive," said Christ.[1]

However, the completion of the negative attitude of renunciation by the positive attitude of affirmation or gift, could not by itself constitute the sole alchemy of spiritual contentment; we also have need of a state of soul that corresponds more directly to happiness properly so called, and this is in the first place and quite obviously the love of God: the sense of the sacred and thus recollection before the Divinity or before a given sacramental expression of its Presence. This is the contemplative beatitude within the sanctuary, and this sanctuary is above all in our heart; for "the kingdom of God is within you."

Another pole of spiritual happiness — complementary to the preceding one — is hope: our conditional certitude of salvation, resulting from our certitude of God and from the sincerity of this certitude. To be really certain of the Absolute, is to draw the operative consequences of this conviction; for the Absolute involves all that we are. Faith demands works; it is not works in themselves which bring about salvation, but they are a part of faith, and faith opens our immortal soul to saving Mercy. Works — or simply "work" in the theological sense — is above all dialogue with Heaven; the moral aura of this alchemy is beauty of soul, hence also the outer activity that manifests it.

---

1. *Acts of the Apostles*, XX, 35. Similarly, Artaxerxes, according to Plutarch: "To give is more royal than to receive."

Happiness is religion and character; faith and virtue. It is a fact that man cannot find happiness within his own limits; his very nature condemns him to surpass himself, and in surpassing himself, to free himself.

*

* *

"I love because I love," said Saint Bernard;[2] this saying indicates the highest reason for our happiness, namely — to repeat — our awareness of the Sovereign Good, and our indefectible attachment to Him who has given us intelligence and immortality.

But there is still more in the saying we have just quoted. Its deepest meaning is: I love because I am Love; which is to say that it refers to the mystery of immanence and union; we would even say: to the mystery of "identity." From this standpoint, our happiness stems from what we are; and we are happy to the extent that we are really and fully ourselves, beyond the husks which, in our ignorance and egoism, we take for our true being. To know oneself is to remember That which is.

---

2. An expression which remotely pertains to the "logic" of the Burning Bush: "I am that I am."

Synthesis and Conclusion

Two enunciations dominate and summarize Vedantic thought: "The world is false, *Brahma* is true"; and "That art thou," namely *Brahma* or *Ātmā*. Perspective of Transcendence in the first case, and perspective of Immanence in the second.

Both ideas express, each in its turn or in its way, the mystery of Unity, the one by expressing Unicity, and the other, Totality; to speak of the one Reality is to say that it is both unique and total. Unity is the aseity — or the quiddity — of the absolutely Real; now when we view the Real in its aspect of Transcendence and in relation to contingencies, it appears as Unicity, for it excludes all that is not it; and when we view it in its aspect of Immanence and in relation to its manifestations, it appears as Totality, for it includes all that manifests it, thus all that exists. On the one hand, the Principle, which is "object" with respect to our cognition, is "above" us, It is transcendent; on the other hand, the Self — since It "thinks" or "projects" our objective existence — is "subject" with respect to this existence and is "within" us, It is immanent. That is, phenomena are either "illusions" veiling Reality, or on the contrary — and the one does not preclude the other — they are "manifestations" which unveil It by prolonging It through an allusive and symbolic language.

To be sure, Transcendence is affirmed a priori by the objective world, whereas Immanence determines above all the subjective world. But this is not to say that Transcen-

221

dence is foreign to the world of subjectivity, and that conversely there is no Immanence in the world of objectivity which surrounds us and to which we belong by our aspect of exteriority. Indeed, Immanence concerns objective phenomena by the fact that they "contain" an existentiating divine Presence, otherwise they could not subsist for an instant; likewise and inversely, Transcendence concerns the subjective microcosm in the sense that the divine Self, essence of all subjectivity, quite obviously remains transcendent with respect to the ego.

It would not be forcing things in any way to say that the mystery of Transcendence refers in a certain manner to the Absolute, while the mystery of Immanence refers to the Infinite; for the elements of rigor, discontinuity or separativity belong incontestably to the first of these two fundamental divine aspects, whereas the elements of gentleness, continuity or unity belong to the second.

The perspective of Transcendence demands that, in the habitual evaluation of phenomena, we not lose sight either of the degrees of reality or of the scale of values; in other words, it demands that our spirit be permeated with the consciousness of the primacy of the Principle; and this finally is the very definition of intelligence. Analogously, the perspective of Immanence demands that we not lose contact with our transpersonal subjectivity which, being the pure Intellect, opens onto the divine Self; and it also demands, *ipso facto*, that we see something of the Self in phenomena, just as, conversely, the perspective of Transcendence demands that we be conscious of the incommensurability, not only between the Principle and manifestation, God and the world, but also between the immanent Self and the ego.

If the transcendent Principle surpasses, extinguishes, excludes or annihilates manifestation, the immanent Self on the contrary attracts, penetrates and reintegrates the ego; not just any ego, but the ego as such, that is, the ego-accident inasmuch as it succeeds in incorporating itself in

222

a sufficient manner into the ego-substance, namely the "inner man" living from the pure Intellect and liberated from the tyranny of illusions.

Taking into account what we would term "typological" affinities, the perspective of Transcendence — which a priori coincides with the "objective" vision of the universe — implies speculative discernment and, by virtue of it, a certain intellective contemplation. In contrast, operative concentration and with it "cardiac" or mystical assimilation, refer, or are related generically, to the perspective of Immanence or to "subjective" realization. In addition we will say that concentration belongs a priori to the will, while discernment belongs to intelligence; two faculties which in their way summarize all of man.

Discernment and contemplation; by analogy we could also say: certitude and serenity. Certitude of thought and serenity of mind first of all, but also certitude and serenity of heart; therefore resulting, not only from the intellectual vision of the Transcendent, but also from the mystical actualization of the Immanent. Realized in the heart, certitude and serenity become respectively unitive faith and contemplative and extinctive recollection;[1] Life and Peace in God and by Him; thus union with God.

The objective perspective, pointing towards Transcendence and the Principle, necessarily opens onto the subjective perspective, pointing towards Immanence and the Self, for the unicity of the object known demands the totality of the knowing subject. One cannot know That which alone is except with all that one is. And this shows and proves that spirituality, in proportion to its profundity and authenticity, can leave nothing outside itself; it

---

1. Faith, not in the sense of simple religious belief or of the pious effort to believe, but in the sense of a quasi-existential assimilation — illuminated *ab intra* — of the doctrinal certitude. It could also be said that recollection is intimately related to the sense of the sacred, as serenity for its part results from the sense of the Transcendent.

encompasses not only truth, but also virtue, and, by extension, art; in a word, all that is human.

Vincit omnia veritas: one ought to add: *Vincit omnia sanctitas.* Truth and Holiness: all values are in these two terms; all that we must love and all that we must be.

INDEX

Index

Index

objectivity of 8
origin of 98

Saint Augustine 17-18, 49, 65, 143,
174, 201
Saint Bernard 200, 220
Saint Paul 54, 71, 106, 141-142, 148,
157
Saint Thomas Aquinas 132, 135, 143,
173
Self, the 71, 87-88, 148-149, 163, 176,
221-223
consciousness of 56
nature of 38-39
vs. the ego 41-43
Shankaracharya 132
Sufism 85, 87, 100, 107, 116, 139, 159,
164-165, 179
the arts in 180
asceticism of 159-164, 169
"average" 161, 169
degrees of 159-172
fideism in 165-166
symbol, symbolism 41-42
and intelligence 124
and *upāya* 157
as language 177
as sacrament 117
exaggerations of 167
geometrical 61-64, 170
interpretations of 118, 166
literary 179-181
morality of 155
of dogmas 124
of duality 63-64
of the heart 172
of quaternity 63-64
of space 42
of trials 217-218
of the triangle 61-64
of wine 179-181
religious 108
universality of 116

tradition 112-113
and esoterism 117
exaggerations of 125, 129-130
inward vs. outward 164-165
transcendence 17, 154, 212, 221-223
transmigration 82-86
truth
and emotion 190, 192
and God 152

and goodness 69
and holiness 224
and humility 209
and hyperbole 176
and Intellect 3
and knowledge 9
and man 145
and morality 111
and salvation 70, 200
and *upāya* 156-157
and virtue 6, 200, 205, 213
as Law 81-82
beauty of 1
literal vs. practical 186
love of 23
metaphysical 11, 115, 161
of Revelation 115
pure 100
relativization of 195-200
symbolic vs. literal 107
totality of 98, 109
universal 117

upāya 131, 156-157, 185

Vedānta 1, 49, 56, 94, 103-104, 118,
121, 165, 221
Virgin Mary 34, 98, 107, 117, 127,
134, 175, 199, 218
virtue
and asceticism 160
and beatitude 202
and discernment 171
and faith 126, 216, 220
and holiness 224
and humility 210-211
and intelligence 203-205, 213
and Law 104
and truth 194
and voluntarism 213
and will 21
as beauty 6, 202, 205
as norm 203
love of 204-206
lucidity of 196, 204
objectivity of 173, 193
science of 200
source of 58-59, 201, 213

Wisdom 32
and knowledge 21
as divine mode 25
perennial 135

229

BY THE SAME AUTHOR

The Transcendent Unity of Religions, *1953*
Revised Edition, *1975, 1984, The Theosophical Publishing House, 1993*

Spiritual Perspectives and Human Facts, *1954, 1969*
New Translation, *Perennial Books, 1987*

Gnosis: Divine Wisdom, *1959, 1978, Perennial Books 1990*

Language of the Self, *1959*
Revised Edition, *World Wisdom Books, 1999*

Stations of Wisdom, *1961, 1980*
Revised Translation, *World Wisdom Books, 1995*

Understanding Islam, *1963, 1965, 1972, 1976, 1979, 1981, 1986, 1989*
Revised Translation, *World Wisdom Books, 1994, 1998*

Light on the Ancient Worlds, *1966, World Wisdom Books, 1984*

In the Tracks of Buddhism, *1968, 1989*
New Translation, Treasures of Buddhism, *World Wisdom Books, 1993*

Logic and Transcendence, *1975, Perennial Books, 1984*

Esoterism as Principle and as Way, *Perennial Books, 1981, 1990*

Castes and Races, *Perennial Books, 1959, 1982*

Sufism: Veil and Quintessence, *World Wisdom Books, 1981*

From the Divine to the Human, *World Wisdom Books, 1982*

Christianity/Islam, *World Wisdom Books, 1985*

The Essential Writings of Frithjof Schuon (S.H. Nasr, Ed.),
1986, Element, 1991

Survey of Metaphysics and Esoterism, *World Wisdom Books, 1986, 2000*

In the Face of the Absolute, *World Wisdom Books, 1989, 1994*

The Feathered Sun: Plain Indians in Art & Philosophy,
World Wisdom Books, 1990

To Have a Center, *World Wisdom Books, 1990*

Roots of the Human Condition, *World Wisdom Books, 1991*

Images of Primordial & Mystic Beauty: Paintings by Frithjof Schuon,
Abodes, 1992

Echoes of Perennial Wisdom, *World Wisdom Books, 1992*

The Play of Masks, *World Wisdom Books, 1992*

Road to the Heart, *World Wisdom Books, 1995*

The Transfiguration of Man, *World Wisdom Books, 1995*

The Eye of the Heart, *World Wisdom Books, 1997*